Revisiting the FHA Appraisal

Dr. J. Craig Julian, SRA, MRICS
Certified General Appraiser in several states

Copyright Information
www.Appraiserscoach.com
Dr. J. Craig Julian, SRA, MRICS
Editor: Lynn M. Julian
Waxhaw, NC 28173,
ISBN 9780615437866

Gratitude

I thank my heavenly Father for the ability to learn and love. I thank my earthly father James L. Julian, III, MAI, SRA for teaching me to never quit learning. I am thankful for my uncle Haynes Hurlock, SREA for paving the way for a great family of appraisers. I also thank my brothers Joe and Mark for challenging me in my appraisal career. I thank Joni Thrasher my big sis for teaching me to think like an appraiser. I thank my nephew Gard for inspiring me early in my career. I also thank my good friend Jim Borowiec for believing in me along the way. I thank my beautiful family: wife: Lynn, daughters Kelsey, Abby, Trinity and Hannah for their incredible love and support. I also want to thank my mom (Claudette Julian) for exhibiting Christ every day when I was growing up. She is a beautiful picture of grace.

Dedication

This book is dedicated to my third daughter: Trinity Elizabeth Julian. You hug me when I am sad, happy, loud and quiet. You invented the word: Imaginate. This means to use your imagination. You are a beautiful butterfly that loves to cuddle. I am blessed to be your dad. Keep imaginating Trinity Bear!

[1] http://www.teachenglishinasia.net/asiablog/asian-water-lilies-and-lotus-flowers

Table of Contents

Revisiting the FHA Appraisal

Introduction: My name is J. Craig Julian and I have been a real property appraiser for 27 years. I have been completing FHA appraisal assignments for 15 years. I earned the SRA (Appraisal Institute) professional appraisal designation in 1988 and MRICS (Royal Institution of Chartered Surveyors) in 2009. I have a degree in real estate as well as other degrees. I love the appraisal of real property and all of the theory encompassed therein. I hope you enjoy this book as much as I enjoyed combining the material into a tangible document.

Intended Use: The intended use of this book is to assist the typical appraiser in completing FHA appraisal assignments.

Intended Users: The intended user of this book is an appraisal student who desires to increase her knowledge regarding completing FHA appraisal assignments.

Design of this book: The design of this book is for the student to work through the chapters. Please read the chapter information and then complete the challenge at the end of the chapter. Then complete the case studies at the end of the book. This will assist the appraiser for working knowledge of FHA appraisal guidelines.

Purpose of the book: Some people may say "why do we need an FHA appraisal book if we have the 4150.20?" That is a fair question. The answer is yes of course we need an FHA book. The FHA document that deals with appraisal standards is the 4150.20. However, FHA has updated their standards for appraisers several times since that document through mortgagee letters. Since FHA has not updated the 4150.20, I felt a need in the marketplace for an FHA book. In this book I have combined the 4150.20 and noted FHA mortgagee letters along with my 27 years experience as a real property appraiser. The 4150.20 and updated mortgagee letters are available under the resources button on www.appraiserscoach.com.   What is a Mortgagee Letter? It is a letter issued by HUD/FHA to inform appraiser's, real estate brokers and mortgage lenders with new rules or revision of old rules in the processing of FHA mortgage loans. If you desire to be updated with FHA Mortgagee Letter's, please send me an email to be placed on a list.

THE APPRAISAL FOUNDATION
Authorized by Congress as the Source of Appraisal Standards and Appraiser Qualifications

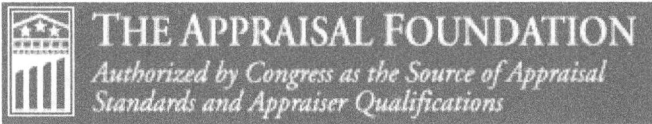

An appraiser according to USPAP/2010/2011 states "one who is expected to perform valuation services competently and in a manner that is independent, impartial and objective." Source: USPAP, Appraisal Foundation.

http://netforum.avectra.com/eWeb/DynamicPage.aspx?Site=TAF&WebCode=HomePage

What is an FHA appraiser?

An FHA appraiser is one that is licensed or certified by in their state and on the FHA appraisal roster. FHA does not demand a test or specifically test to complete FHA appraisal assignments; however, the competency provision does require the appraiser to disclose if he is not competent to complete the requested report. Therefore, I recommend taking a FHA appraisal course to prepare you for these types of assignments. I teach FHA courses every month, plus please check my website for a class near you. Please read the next statement is it was one of the most important statements from FHA in the past 25 years!

Major Changes to FHA Appraisal: 2005-ML-48

In a continuing effort to reform and standardize its appraisal requirements, FHA has shifted from its historical emphasis on the repair of in or property deficiencies and now only requires repairs for those property conditions that rise above the level of cosmetic defects, minor defects or normal wear and tear. The key to completing FHA appraisals are the three S's. These include safety, soundness and security.

Safety relates to the occupants of the improvements. If you believe that something is a safety concern for the occupants or proposed occupants, then you would make the appraisal report subject to the repair or replacement of the item. Missing hand rails may or may not be a safety concern. We will discuss this issue and others at great length.

Soundness relates to the structure and structural components of the dwelling. They include not only the foundation but also other elements such as floor, wall and roof framing systems. Decks, porches and patios may also pose structural issues due to improper construction or deteriorated condition. Site conditions may also impact soundness.

Security relates to the financial risk to the insurance company which in this case is HUD/FHA. FHA is concerned about the marketability of the property. As you know, properties will marginal locations can be difficult to market. For example, if a house sides to a busy intersection, it may be very difficult to market. This next photo is a great example of what can happen to houses near busy streets and rail road tracks.

2

---

2 http://news.webshots.com/photo/1542453896084327267SfFJsl

Chapter One – Overview of FHA Appraisals:

FHA is known as the Federal Housing Administration. This group commonly known as FHA is managed by HUD (Department of Housing and Urban Development). It began in 1934 and has insured more than 35 million properties. The original purpose of FHA was to assist low income with their real estate home purchase; however, loan limits have risen to assist the middle class as well. FHA is the only agency of the government that operates totally from its self generated income with no cost to the taxpayer. FHA insures mortgage loans, therefore, the underwriter, appraiser and processor must be specially trained to complete FHA assignments.

How do I become an FHA Appraiser?

I am so glad that you asked. I personally would type FHA appraisal application on a Google search or you could type in the following:
http://www.hud.gov/offices/hsg/sfh/appr/_rost.cfm

How do I determine if I was approved as an FHA appraiser?

You can try the following:

https://entp.hud.gov/idapp/html/apprlook.cfm or yes, you guessed it, type in FHA approved appraiser roster on a Google search and you will find the right link.

How and where do I receive FHA appraisal assignments?

The process for receiving an appraisal assignment is as follows:
1. The lender (bank, credit union, savings and loan, pawn shop) selects the appraiser from the FHA appraiser roster.
2. The lender assigns the appraiser to the FHA case file.

3. The lender submits an FHA case number to the appraiser via fax, e-mail, regular mail, stone tablets, etc.
4. The appraiser will begin the appraisal process. (Be sure to include the FHA case number on each page of the appraisal report. It belongs on the top right hand corner).

Who can I communicate with regarding the FHA appraisal?

I am so glad you are asking such great questions. Let me answer.
1. The appraiser should not discuss the appraisal request with anyone other than the underwriter or directed staff.
2. If the appraiser has questions on how to proceed on an FHA appraisal request, they must be directed by the underwriter.

What about FHA appraisal fees?

My personal recommendation is that higher fees lead to better stuff for the appraiser. Seriously, fees are negotiated between the client and the appraiser. This is a business decision; however, please keep in mind that FHA appraisals have a different scope of work than Fannie Mae. Therefore, I recommend that you consider the extra work required.

How will FHA monitor the appraisal process?

Another great question!

FHA monitors the appraisal process as follows:

1. HUD/FHA will spot check appraisal reports for factual data. This is completed through periodic reviews.

2. HUD/FHA will also check your report for completeness. They want a complete report the first time. They do not want to contact you several times and you finally complete the report on the 3rd try.

3. HUD/FHA does not want you to ask for repair conditions that are unnecessary. They want you to comply with their guidelines. Some appraisers will say "I am conservative by nature" and will ask for repairs to be safe". This is not what FHA desires. They want you to follow their guidelines. In fact, USPAP is very clear about not being biased. If you are conservative, then you could be biased and that is a violation. Most of all FHA wants you to use sound judgment.

4. FHA/HUD expects you to maintain your state appraisal license/certification in good standing. You will need to notify them if it lapses.

5. If an FHA field appraiser contacts you for amendments to your report. They expect you to be professional, courteous and prompt with an amendment.

FHA Loan Types

There are several types of FHA loans that can be made. These include

the following:

FHA/203B

The 203B is the typical loan sought by the majority of homeowners seeking an FHA loan. They require a minimum 3% down payment.

203H

The 203H is the FHA loan for disaster victims. These types of loans are available in designated disaster areas.

255HECM Home equity loans

The 255HECM is designed for people desiring to borrow money based on the equity in their house.

203K

The 203K loan is designed for properties that need some type of rehabilitation. This work can vary from minor repairs to major renovation. For example, a purchaser would like to add an exercise room and is doing an FHA loan. The appraiser would appraise the property "as completed". Of course as the FHA appraiser, you would need a copy of any documents that indicate the design, square footage and materials planed for the exercise room. The minimum loan amount is $5,000 with no maximum.

203K Streamline (Mortgage Letter 2005-50)

The 203K streamline is similar to the 203K; however, there is no minimum loan amount. The maximum loan amount is $35,000 in repair money. There is a 6 month maximum escrow period, thus repairs have to be completed within 180 days. This program cannot be utilized for structural repairs; therefore, if these type of repairs are necessary would need to use the regular 203K.

Energy Efficient Mortgage (EEM)

This program is to be used with other FHA loan programs. A borrower can receive a loan up to $8,000. The program will loan a borrower money to make a home more energy efficient.

The following requirements are for completing REO appraisal reports.

REO Appraisals (Mortgagee Letter's 2000-27 and 2006-09)

1. HUD is the owner.
2. Intended Use is to provide an "as is" value of the foreclosed property for marketing and bidding purposes.
3. Some REO properties with more than $5,000 of repairs will be eligible for Section 203K, renovation program.
4. Use market driven sales as always. So, if there are a few REO properties, you would not use those; however, if the REO sales are prevalent, then use those.

Who should the appraisal be addressed to?

Client: Lender/Client: HUD/FHA.

What forms do I use again?

1. Single Family Residence -URAR/Form 1004 (This includes Modular)

2. Condominium Unit or Townhouse with amenities Form 1073

3. 2-4 Family or Small Residential Income Property - Form 1025

4. Manufactured Housing - Form 1004 C

FHA/HUD Certifications

FHA/HUD would like for you to make additional certifications in addition to the preprinted certifications on the 1004 form.

1. I inspected the attic of the subject property with a visual inspection. This included a visual inspection up to my chest.
2. I inspected the crawl space of the subject property with a visual inspection. This included a visual inspection up to my chest.
3. Based on my visual observations as a real property appraiser, the subject property meets the minimum property requirements (MPR) as prescribed by HUD/FHA.

What about this practice of always completing the appraisal report subject

to?

This was the normal practice until December 19, 2005; however, as stated in the

Mortgagee letter 2005-ML-48, "FHA has shifted from its historical emphasis on

the repair of minor property deficiencies and now only requires repairs for those

property conditions that rise above the level of cosmetic defects, minor defects or normal wear and tear. FHA Roster Appraisers are reminded to report all readily observable property deficiencies, as well as any adverse conditions discovered performing the research involved in completing the appraisal, within the appraisal reporting form." Thus, the majority of appraisal reports performed for FHA will be completed "as is".

Now what?

Now that you are on the FHA appraiser roster and have your first assignment, how in the world do you complete an FHA appraisal assignment? Some will answer that you follow the 4150.20, others will answer that you use the VC sheets, some will answer that you complete them much like you do VA and finally others will say that you do them like Fannie Mae reports. The truth is FHA appraisal assignments are different from Fannie, Freddie, and VA. So, please read on so that you can become informed and competent to perform FHA appraisal assignments. We will start with the updates for FHA that occurred over the past 24 months.

Chapter Two: *What is new with FHA Appraisal?*

The first few items are not actually new as they were derived from a 2000

Mortgagee Letter; however, I wanted to mention these since they are still

relevant.

· Failing to make a complete interior and exterior visual inspection of the subject property and a visual inspection of the exterior and each comparable; to take required photographs and to provide maps. (USPAP Manual Standard 2 & HUD)

FHA requires that the appraiser of record inspect the subject property's

interior and exterior. She must also inspect the exterior of the comparable sales

from the street. Front/side and rear/side photographs of the subject property are

required as well. The front of each comparable sale is required and the appraiser

should not utilize the MLS photographs. If you use MLS photographs, please

explain within the report the reason for using MLS photographs. A location map

with the subject and comparable sales indicated is required as well. The sketch

should include the floor-plan of the subject property including the garage,

basement, patio, porch and any storage buildings. Measurements are also

required on the sketch. The intended user of the report must be able to replicate

the GLA indicated by the appraiser. I am including an FHA appraisal checklist in this book that covers all of the items required for a proper FHA appraisal

inspection. This checklist is located in chapter five of this book. [3]

· **Failing to include sufficient information to enable users of the appraisal to understand the report properly. (USPAP & HUD 4150.2 6 4-1.)**

This requirement would be judged based on what your peers would do in a

similar situation. For example, if the subject property backs to a shopping center,

then the appraiser should disclose this issue in the report. Additionally, the

appraiser must decide if this issue affects the value or marketability. The

appraiser should base this decision on acceptable appraisal methodology, not

rules of thumb. [4]

---

[3] http://www.hud.gov/offices/adm/hudclips/letters/mortgagee/2000ml.cfm
[4] Ibid.

· Failing to report limiting conditions that affect the appraisal, such as but not limited to, proximity to a municipal landfill, pending zone changes, necessary repairs. (USPAP Manual Standard 2-2(b)(viii) & HUD 4150.2 6 4-1H, 5-1A(3).)

This of course is a USPAP issue and could become a legal issue for the

appraiser if not handled properly. USPAP requires the appraiser to be very clear

in regard to limiting conditions. If the appraiser neglects to place a limiting

condition or is not clear in regard to what they are attempting to disclose through

limiting conditions, then the appraiser could have legal liability. Therefore, the

appraiser is cautioned to be careful when using limiting conditions. Of course the

other issue is the fact that FHA requires the appraiser to disclose if the subject

has an atypical location such as being located close to an airport, landfill, or if

deferred maintenance is indicated. The key is disclosure.

[5]

---

[5] http://www.uptownupdate.com/2010/09/another-mcjunkin-building-zoning-change.html

· Failing to report the highest and best use of the property. (USPAP Manual Standard 2-1, 2-2 & HUD 4150.2 6 2-1M.)

Of course USPAP requires the appraiser to report the highest and best use; however, practically speaking, how can an appraiser complete an appraisal without knowing the highest and best use? This will lead to questions regarding land value, total value and remaining economic life.

If this is your subject property, you have a land appraisal. If this is one of your comparable sales, then you will need to consider highest and best use, land values, remaining economic life, etc.

---

[6] http://news.bbc.co.uk/2/hi/uk_news/england/north_yorkshire/8101926.stm

· **Failing to recognize readily observable adverse conditions, such as but not limited to, termite/insect damage, hazardous materials, soil contamination, poor drainage or ventilation, defective construction, fire or flood damage, or the presence of defective paint surfaces for pre-1978 homes. (USPAP Manual Standard 1-3 & HUD 4150.2 6 3-6A.)**

The FHA appraiser has a slightly different scope of work than the assignment that she completed under Fannie or Freddie guidelines. Therefore, the appraiser must check for items such as leaking toilets, cracking, chipping or peeling paint on house built prior to 1978. The appraiser should also check for hazardous materials, soil contamination and poor drainage. For a complete FHA appraisal checklist, please read the section labeled as such.

Good rule of thumb, if there are fire fighters in the attic cleaning up, the house probably had a fire!

· **Property not connected to adequate public or individual water supply and sewage disposal. (HUD 4150.2 6 3-6A(5).)**

The appraiser should verify that the subject property has water and sewer connections. She can verify that it is adequate by turning on the water at the faucet and checking for water pressure. The following is a layout of a well and septic system. We are not required to provide a layout; however, we do need to discuss in the report.

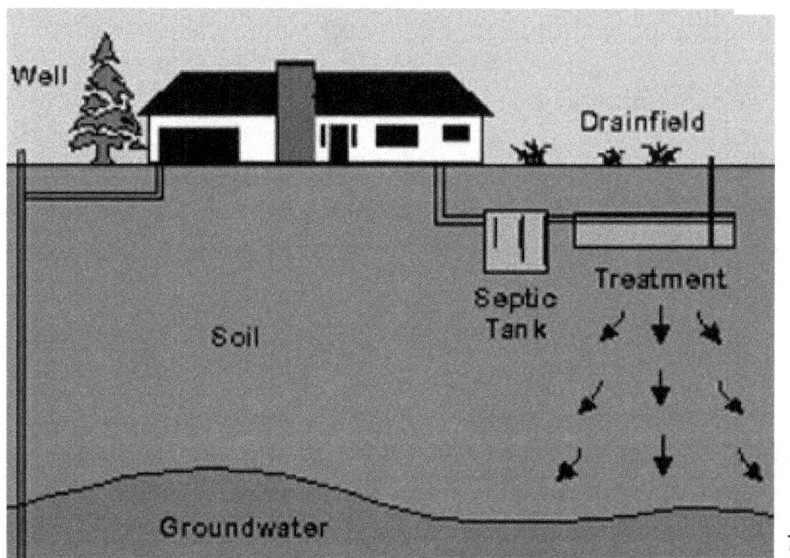

[7] http://www.marioncountyhealthdept.org/SubSurfaceSystem.html

· Failing to report roof has signs of leaking or excessive wear. (USPAP Manual Standard 2-2(b)(iii), HUD 4150.2 6 3-6 (12).)

The appraiser should report the condition of the roof. If the roof has at least two years remaining economic life, then the appraiser will have anything to report regarding the roof. If the roof has less than two years of remaining economic life, then you should make the appraisal report subject to a new roof.

How is this roof?

· Obvious electrical inadequacies, such as but not limited to, observable frayed wiring. (HUD4150.2 6 3-6)

These are safety issues. If the subject property has electrical inadequacies, then the appraiser must report these items on the appraisal report. If the appraiser detects frayed wiring, missing electrical outlets, etc. Then make the appraisal report subject to repair. Safety first, the business should be second.

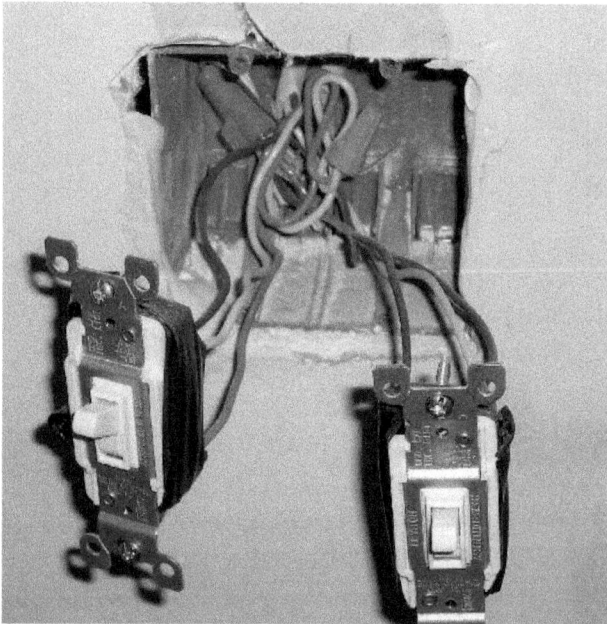

· Failing to renew appraisal license or certification (HUD 4150.2 6 7-1I & NHA Section 202(e).)

An appraiser must have a current appraisal license in the state where she is providing appraisal assignments.

· Failing to report to HUD any state or local disciplinary action within last 2 years that relates to an appraisal report performed by the appraiser. (HUD 4150.2 6 7-1I.)

The appraiser must report to HUD/FHA any state or local disciplinary action

within the last 2 years of application.

· Not having a temporary appraisal license or not operating under a reciprocal agreement. (HUD 4150.2 6 7-1I.)

An appraiser must have a current appraisal license in the state where she is

providing appraisal assignments.

· Failing to report to HUD any disciplinary action that results in the suspension of the appraiser within 14 days of such action. (HUD 4150.2 6 7-1I(2).)

The appraiser must disclose to HUD/FHA if she receives discipline in the form of

suspension of an appraisal license.

Now for the major updates that have occurred over the past 24 months.

Requirement	Implication	Source: ML/FAQ
1004MC Form	This form is required for all mortgage transactions. I have written a book and course that covers this form. My best advice is to report several years of sales that can be used as a supplement to the form. In addition, FHA requires the appraiser to include an absorption rate analysis. This analysis can assist the appraiser in developing a marketing time for the area. 1. If the market is declining, please provide two closed sales within 90 days of the effective date of the appraisal. 2. Please provide two current listings or pending sales that supplement the closed sales. Consider adjusting the listings based on the list to sales price ratio.	ML: 2009-09
1004MC Form	Does the 1004MC Form have to match the neighborhood section of the report? No, The neighborhood section reflects the whole market and the 1004MC should reflect competitive properties.	2010 Valuation Protocol
Verification of data	The appraiser must verify the sale with a disinterested third party. This can mean contacting a broker or checking the county records for closed	ML 2009-09

Revisiting the FHA Appraisal, 1.0, 01/01/2011, JCJ, No Single or complete part of this workbook can be reprinted or duplicated in any way without the permission of Dr. J. Craig Julian, SRA, MRICS. If you have any questions regarding this material please e-mail craigjulian@gmail.com.

	sales. FHA requires the data sources to be available for replication. This means a reviewer can confirm the sales the appraiser used in her report.	
Appraiser Independence	1. Prohibition of mortgage brokers and commission based lender staff from the appraisal process. 2. Appraisers may place the fee received for the assignment within the report without recourse. The fee shall not include a AMC or lender add on fee. 3. Appraisers must be paid reasonable and customary fees for the area. 4. Fees charged by the AMC must be separate from the appraisal fee and also must be reasonable and customary for the area.	ML 2009-28
Appraiser Engagement	Appraisers must be competent to complete the assignment as required by USPAP. Specifically, appraisers must have market knowledge of the area when completing the appraisal for FHA loan purposes. They specifically state the following regarding competency: The appraiser must have ready access to sources for market data such as MLS. Familiarity with the market by way of actual	ML 2009-28

	field experience in and working knowledge of the market. Experience in the property type being valued. Educational qualifications for the assignment being completed. In regard to appraisal fees, a borrower can pay for the appraisal fee directly to the appraiser. However, FHA has not set appraisal fees for appraisers at this time.	
Appraisal Portability	The appraiser completes the report for Bank of America and now the borrower has changed lenders. The appraiser is not required to do anything else.	ML 2009-29
Second Appraisals for FHA	Occasionally a lender will require a second FHA appraisal. This can be completed if there were material deficiencies in the first report. Also, if the first appraiser was on the lender's exclusionary list, a second report can be ordered.	ML 2009-29
Case number assignment date	The appraisal inspection date can proceed the case number assignment date as long as there are notes in the FHA Connection regarding who performed the appraisal assignment.	ML 2009-29
Appraisal Validity Period	FHA appraisal reports are valid for 120 days and should not be completed for FHA loan purposes until the time is ended.	ML 2009-30
Certified Appraisers	As of 10/01/2009, all appraisal reports must be	ML 2009-36

Only	completed by a certified appraiser for FHA loan purposes.	
Flood Map Required	A flood map is required for all properties that are located in the Special Flood Hazard Area. For new construction: If any part of the property improvements is located in a SFHA, the property is ineligible for FHA mortgage insurance. Your job as an appraiser is to report what you believe, not reject properties. Existing properties can still be insured for FHA mortgage insurance. Manufactured homes must be located above the flood area for FHA mortgage insurance purposes.	ML 2009-37
Appraisal Performance standards and sanctions	Appraisers may be warned, required to complete education, removed, prohibited from performing appraisal assignments, sued under civil or criminal law, removed or lose standing as an FHA appraiser for violating FHA appraisal requirements.	ML 2009-41
FAQ's for 2009	Property is under construction, but more than 90% complete with minor finish work required. Appraiser will make the report "subject to the following repairs…" The final inspection can be completed by anyone the lender selects in this case.	2009 Valuation Protocol
Wood Destroying Insects (Termites and	Inspections are required for the following reasons: 1. Mandated by local or state	2009/2010 Valuation Protocol

other critters)	jurisdictions.	
	2. Customary for the area: The lender will advise if an inspection is required. They have access to a website that indicates probability of infestation.	
	3. If repairs are required, an underwriter may waive the repairs at their discretion. This is a reminder that the lender is responsible to make loan decisions. Additionally, the lender can research TIP's (Termite Infestation Probability) if they are not familiar with the area. It is the appraiser's job to report what we view at the property.	
Utilities – Well and Septic	The appraiser is not required to sketch the distances between the well and septic ; however, he or she should be mindful of FHA's minimum distance requirement between private wells and sources of pollution (septic systems) in the performance of FHA appraisals; and, if discernible comment on them. Prudent appraisal practice	2009/2010 Valuation Protocol

| | would have the appraiser requesting a copy of a survey from the homeowner, if available. It is not mandatory that the appraiser show the distance to the lot lines on the sketch as well. If the lender determines there is a need to confirm the distances between the well and septic, they should consult a third party. This third party could be an appraiser if he/she is competent to make such a determination. If public water is available, the appraiser should make a note in the appraisal report. The lender will decide if the property is required to connect to public utilities. Water tests are required if the appraiser notes a problem or if required by state/local authorities. Dug wells are acceptable if a survey is completed by an engineer. A well can be located in the basement if it is allowed by local authority. For new construction, it is not allowed in arctic or sub-arctic regions. The appraiser will note if a property has public water available. The lender will determine if it is a requirement for closing. Shared wells are acceptable up to four properties; however, there must be a shared well agreement for the well. | |
| Inspections on | Oil Tanks: An inspection of an (UST) underground | 2009/2010 |

various items	storage tank does not automatically trigger a certification. Testing is required when the appraiser notes any readily observable evidence of on-site contamination. I would say "if the people or pets are glowing, then I would require an inspection". Seriously, make the report subject to if you see or smell a problem.	Valuation Protocol
Inspections on various items	Who can complete the CIR? (Compliance Inspection Report). The lender can order this from anyone they chose if the repair condition is noted from the appraisal.	2009/2010 Valuation Protocol
Inspections on various items	Engineer's report (certification) is still required for manufactured homes.	2009 Valuation Protocol
Inspections on various items	Can an appraiser complete a final inspection? Yes, the lender selects the person to complete the final inspection.	2009 Valuation Protocol
Inspections on various items	Can the DE (direct endorsement) underwriter waive cosmetic repairs? Yes.	2009/2010 Valuation Protocol
Repairs	Is the appraiser required to give an estimate of repairs? Yes, repair estimates are required for those items that may represent a risk to the health and safety of the occupants and/or the soundness or structural integrity of the property. The appraiser must indicate the extent of the repairs and note this	2010 Valuation Protocol

	in the appropriate section of the appraisal, or in the additional comments section. The estimated cost to cure is noted together with the required repairs.	
Inspection	Can the 1004D be used in lieu of form HUD 92051 for manufactured housing? No, manufacturing housing, whether new or existing, requires the use of HUD form 92051. The 1004D can be used only for existing site built construction (stick built or modular).	2010 Valuation Protocol
Cost Approach	Cost Approach: The cost approach is required when it is necessary for credible results. It should be used for unique properties with specialized improvements, new manufactured housing or if the client requires. The square footage method is to be used and addressed in the cost approach section. The 1007 form is not required, but also not retired. It is required when valuing property on tribal land trust's, Native American Program or on leased land as found on Hawaiian lands.	2009/2010 Valuation Protocol
Cost Approach	Estimated Remaining Economic Life: it is still required for completing FHA appraisal reports. On a Condominium (1073 Form), place the remaining economic life in the reconciliation section. The comment can be stated as follows: "Estimated	2009/2010 Valuation Protocol

	Remaining Economic Life _____ years."	
Property Type	Accessory Dwelling Unit: An ADU is separate living area from the primary residence that typically includes a kitchen, bathroom and sleeping areas. It can include a garage apartment that may or may not be attached to the primary residence. The appraiser is responsible for determining if it is considered a second dwelling. This is done based on highest and best use. The number of meters does not conclude that it is a second dwelling.	2009/2010 Valuation Protocol
Property Type	Manufactured House being used for storage. This is acceptable if is not a safety hazard and is allowed by local jurisdiction and is not functioning as a living unit. If valued, the appraiser must give a contributory value as a storage building, not as a living unit.	2009 Valuation Protocol
Property Type	Manufactured Housing: Is vinyl skirting attached to framework acceptable? There must be a perimeter enclosure constructed of concrete, masonry or treated wood. Light weight, non-load bearing skirting may be attached over the perimeter enclosure but is not an acceptable substitute.	2010 Valuation Protocol
Property Type	Two unit property: FHA does accept two unit properties comprised on two detached or	2009 Valuation Protocol

	unattached dwellings on one property provided it is a single real estate entity having a legal use.	
Property Type	HECM (Home Equity Conversion Mortgage) appraisals are completed the same way as regular FHA appraisals.	2009 Valuation Protocol
Lender Concerns	Handrails and Trip Hazards: Hand rails are not required if they do not constitute a safety risk. The lender has discretion on whether to require hand rails.	2009/2010 Valuation Protocol
Lender Concerns	Lead based paint: Any area of the improvements painted with lead based paint (prior to 1978) that has physical deficiencies must be repaired prior to closing. The appraiser would make the appraisal subject to repair of the deficiency. If there is no deficiency, then the appraiser can note that the house was built prior to 1978 without any noted problem. Special Note: On April 22, 2010, the EPA changed its requirements regarding renovation, repair and painting for houses built prior to 1978. Homeowners can do their own repair. If the property is a rental, the person doing the painting must be certified and follow lead-safe work practices required by the rule. Contractors who perform the repair must be certified and must follow	2009/2010 Valuation Protocol

	specific work practices to prevent lead contamination. Who Can inspect for completion of repairs when the appraiser noted defective paint in a home built prior to 1978? FHA Appraisers and Inspectors are allowed to inspect if the repair was completed, but not compliance with the EPA rule. What documentation will be required to satisfy the EPA rule? The lender will require the homeowner to certify they complied with the EPA rule and if work was completed by a contractor, then the lender will require a copy of the certification. This part does not include the appraiser, so we do not have to worry about this section. Our part consist of making sure the repairs were completed.	
Lender Concerns	Private Road Maintenance Agreement: FHA does not require evidence of a private road maintenance agreement; however, they do require an easement. The appraiser should ask if a maintenance agreement exists and comment on the condition of the private road, especially if it is in inferior condition.	2009 Valuation Protocol
Lender Concerns	Garage door opener: FHA no longer requires repair of a garage door opener; however, local requirements may require repair. I would make a	2009 Valuation Protocol

	note in the report regarding the garage door opener if found to be faulty.	
Lender Concerns	Fall Distance of High Voltage Transmission Lines: FHA will insure a loan of a house if the property improvements are not located within the tower's fall distance. In addition, the improvements must not be located within the easement of the easement. The appraiser should comment on the easement, fall distance and whether it will have an effect the marketability.	2009 Valuation Protocol
Lender Concerns	Remaining Economic Life: The appraiser must report the remaining economic life. If the economic life is less than the loan term, FHA will reject the property for loan insurance purposes. The appraiser will need to comment when the remaining economic life is less than 30 years. In addition, if there is a significant difference between the effective age and the actual age, an explanation is required.	2009 Valuation Protocol
Reconsideration of Value	The underwriter's lender can request a reconsideration of value. The underwriter can send information that was available, but not used in the appraisal report. The appraiser must consider the data; however, they are not required to change	2010 Valuation Protocol

	their value opinion. The appraiser should address the information presented in a reply. The reply could be presented in an email, letter or the appraisal report if applicable. The appraiser may not charge for a reconsideration of value since the data presented would have been available at the time of the appraisal. The appraiser may not consider data that has closed after the effective date of the appraisal. FHA does not accept retrospective appraisal reports.	
Use of Trainee's	FHA does not accept appraiser trainee's. A trainee can do some work and be noted in the report; however, he/she cannot sign the report.	2010 Valuation Protocol
Can the 2055 form be used for a second appraisal?	No. If a second appraisal is required by the lender, the 1004 form must be used.	2010 Valuation Protocol
Distressed Sales	Can FHA Roster appraisers use foreclosures, short sales and other distressed sales? If these sales are prevalent, then the appraiser should use them. If not prevalent, then use "normal sales".	2010 Valuation Protocol
Conversion of a VA/Conventional appraisal to FHA.	Can a VA or conventional appraisal be converted to an FHA appraisal? Yes, as long as the scope of work was the same when the appraisal was completed. As you know, the main difference is the	2010 Valuation Protocol

	inspection. The inspection must be completed as though it was an FHA appraisal.	
Seller Concessions	Do not adjust the subject for sales concessions. However, you may need to adjust the comparable sales for concessions if the sale sold for more than other sales without concessions. For example, if the seller paid $10,000 in closing cost on behalf of the buyer and this sale sold for $10,000 more than competing properties, then this sale requires an adjustment.	

What happens if I violate an FHA guidelines or policy?

FHA/HUD has the following options:

1. They can send the appraisal report in question into the state appraisal board.

2. They can fine you up to $10,000 per false claim plus treble damages suffered by by the government.

3. HUD/FHA can send the appraisal report to the professional appraisal organization that holds your membership.

4. HUD/FHA can impose criminal sanctions against you as an appraiser.

What about the beloved VC (Valuation Condition) sheets? The answer is that they were retired as of December 19, 2005 (Mortgagee letter dated 2005-ML-48). Thus, some FHA documents still reference the VC sheets, but they are officially retired.

Quiz Time

1. Do I reject a house if it is not hooked up to public utilities and they are available?

2. HUD/FHA expects me to deduct all seller concessions when they are paid by the seller: – T or F.

3. HUD expects you to be conservative when completing appraisal assignments – T or F.

4. HUD/FHA expects you to error on the side of caution in regard to repairs

   T or F.

Next, we will discuss what items lead to an automatic repair for FHA standards. Some of these items have changed over the years, so please forget what you know about automatic FHA repairs and learn what is current today.

Chapter Three

FHA Appraisal Repair Items – (Subject To)

What items lead to an automatic repair again? There was a time when appraisers had more control of the repair process for FHA. Today, the ultimate decision is made by the underwriter, not the appraiser. The appraiser will make reports subject to when certain items or situations are present. Let's take a look at these items and do note that the list is much smaller than in the past.

Examples of property conditions that may represent a risk to the health and safety of the occupants or the soundness of the property for which FHA will continue to require **automatic** repair for existing properties include, but are not limited to:

Inadequate access/egress from bedrooms to exterior of home.

Every bedroom must have a window that leads to the exterior. If there are security bars, they must have a quick release button.

[8]

---

[8] http://www.alltexexteriors.com/security/

Revisiting the FHA Appraisal, 1.0, 01/01/2011, JCJ, No Single or complete part of this workbook can be reprinted or duplicated in any way without the permission of Dr. J. Craig Julian, SRA, MRICS. If you have any questions regarding this material please e-mail craigjulian@gmail.com.

Leaking or worn out roofs (if 3 or more layers of shingles on leaking or worn out roof, all existing shingles must be removed before re-roofing.)
Thus, a new roof is required any time that you have 3 or more layers of shingles

on a leaking roof. Also, if the roof does not have 2 years of remaining economic

life, then it must be replaced as well.

How is this roof?

9

How about this roof?

10

9 http://oldstersview.wordpress.com/2008/05/09/

Evidence of structural problems (such as foundation damage caused by excessive settlement)

So, if the foundation is not performing the job for which it is intended, then the

appraiser will make the appraisal subject to a structural inspection. This is not a

situation that happens very often, in fact it is a rare occurrence.

11

If the crack is large enough to put my hand into, then it is a problem.

---

[10] http://www.donsradiomuseum.com/distractions.htm

[11] http://activerain.com/blogsview/393781/question-when-is-a-crack-in-brick-veneer-too-large-

Defective interior/exterior paint surfaces in homes constructed pre-1978.

In any home built prior to 1978, the appraiser should be very careful. FHA/HUD is very serious about lead based paint. In reality all paint has some lead; however, homes built prior to 1978 had excessive amounts of lead in the paint. Therefore, if you are appraising a house built prior to 1978, then you must watch for cracking, peeling and flaking paint. If you note the paint to be cracking, peeling or flaking, then it should be made subject to repair.

12

---

12 http://www.finehousepainters.com/pagina.asp?id=4

Active wood destroying Insects present or if mandated by the state or local jurisdiction or at lender's discretion.

If the subject property has active wood destroying insects, then this issue must be remedied. Additionally, if an inspection is required by the lender, state or local government, then it is required.

13

---

13 http://defendertermiteandpestcontrol.com/services/termite-services/

Inspection on water well if appraiser notes one of the following: 1. Corrosion of pipes (plumbing), 2. areas of intense ag, coal mining, dump, junkyard, landfill, factory, gas station (all within ¼ mile). If the appraiser notes corrosive piping in a water well system, then this situation must be repaired. In areas of intense ag, coal mining, dump yard, junkyard, landfill, factory, industrial parks, or gas stations, then the water well will need to be inspected by a licensed professional.

14

---

[14] http://www.bushman.cc/corrosion_photos.html

Inspection of private sewer if appraiser notes system failure, or if mandated by state or local jurisdiction or at lender's discretion.

Additional comments regarding the water well and septic tank:

Well must be a minimum of 50' from the septic tank, 100' from septic drain field (if local code allows), 10' from property line (if adjacent property is commercial), and 25' from house. [15]

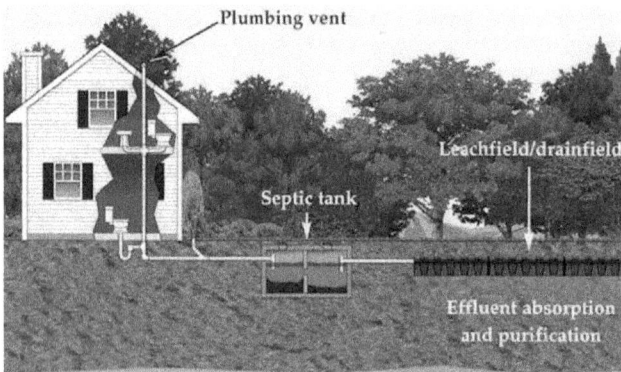

Septic tank

Water well

[15] Appendix D 4150.2 FHA/HUD Hudclips

Standing water against the foundation and/or excessively damp basements.

If water is standing against the foundation, then grading will be required to elevate this drainage problem. Also, if water is standing in the basement or excessive dampness is evident, then this issue will need to be corrected. Thus, make the appraisal report subject to curing the issue.

16

16

http://www.waterdamagelocal.com/education/north_carolina/fayetteville/basement_water_damage/fayetteville_nc_basement_water_damage.aspx

Hazardous materials on the site or within the improvements. These include toxic waste, car batteries, old tires, uncle Buck, etc.

17

Faulty or defective mechanical systems (electrical, plumbing, or heating). If any of these items have failed, then it is an automatic repair. For example, if the electrical system is not performing properly, then it must be repaired. If the toilet is leaking, it must be repaired. However, if the faucet is leaking, but **NOT** creating damage, then it will not have to be repaired. If the heating is not performing as designed, then it will need to be repaired.

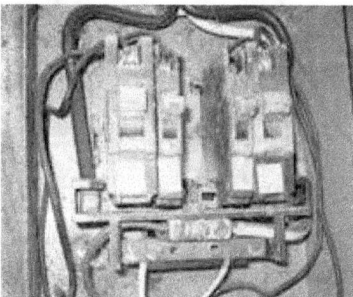

18

---

17 http://www.pennysaveronline.com/classified/ads/farm/
18 http://www.ci.pg.ca.us/cdd/ehrl.htm

Evidence of possible structural failure: settlement or bulging foundation wall.

So, if the foundation is not performing the job for which it is intended, then the appraiser will make the appraisal subject to a structural inspection. This is not a situation that happens very often, in fact it is a rare occurrence.

19

If the flooring is a hazard or soiled with urine.

The flooring must be free of hazards and unhealthy contamination. This can be caused by unruly children, pets or plain messy people.

---

[19] http://www.jacksonvillefoundationrepair.com/

Lack of an all weather road.

If you cannot gain access to the property in all four seasons, then this is an automatic repair. This includes the road to the subject as well as the driveway for the subject property. The road/driveway can be gravel, concrete, asphalt, etc. Just make sure it is all weather. Little Timmy needs to be able to get home in time to feed lassie.

20

You need an all weather road to the subject property. This road will not get you home in time to make dinner.

---

20 http://www.fs.fed.us/r1/clearwater/rap/index.htm

Case Study Challenge

Case Study 1

Based on the following photo, would this road pass the test?

Case Study 2

Based on the following photo, would you make a note or complete the report

subject to?

[21]

---

[21] http://www.nachi.org/forum/f16/brick-issues-42201/

Case Study 3

Based on the following photo, would you make it to subject to or just note the item in the report?

22

---

22 http://www.homerepairhandyman.com/project/dormer_window_wood_siding_repair

Chapter Four –FHA Appraisals: Make a statement.

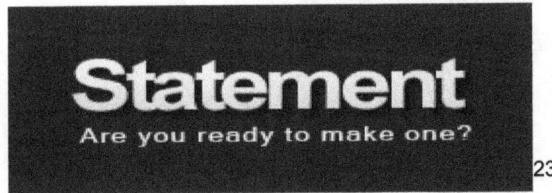

The following items should be **noted** in the appraisal report, but **not required**. When in doubt, note the issue and let the DE underwriter aware of the issue. FHA does not require these items as automatic repairs; however, if the item becomes a safety, soundness or sanitary issue, then you will make the appraisal subject to repair. Let's work through these issues one at a time. Remember the key is sound judgment.

Missing handrails

This issue surprises appraisers, but FHA made a change to their requirements that affected the handrail issue. They no longer require hand rails. This may be fine if the stairs are 2 feet off the ground; however, this requires sound judgment from the appraiser. My personal opinion is if a wood deck is 3 feet off the ground with no handrails, then I would require they be installed. Additionally, if handrails are missing on a stairway that is located on a two story house, then I would require those to be installed as well.

[23] http://www.blogohblog.com/wordpress-theme-statement/

24

Hey! Where did the handrail go?

Let's take a look at another one or two:

The first one seemed okay at first glance; however, when you take a look at the walkway, it is a safety concern.

25

---

24 http://ths.gardenweb.com/forums/load/decor/msg0714143231359.html
25 http://inspectorjoe.activerain.com/archives/2009/1

26

I would make this one subject to as well. The bottom steps seem okay, but the

guard rails are missing. That is a safety concern in my mind.

Let's try one more:

27

---

26 Ibid.

27 http://www.inspectapedia.com/interiors/Basement_Stairs.htm

Now, let's discuss other potential concerns.

Cracked or damaged exit doors that are otherwise operable.

So the exit door is slightly damaged, but still functions as a door. No problem, make a note, take a photo and write about the issue in the report. Again, if the item rises to the level of a health and safety issue, then it should be repaired.

Cracked window glass

If you note that a window has a crack, but still functions as a window, then make a note, take a photo and write about it in the report.

28

---

[28] http://www.mountain-glass.com/services.php

Would you make this subject to? I would.

Defective paint surfaces in homes constructed post 1978

If the subject property has cracking, peeling or chipping paint and was built in 1978 and after, then make a note, take a photo and write about it in the report. If the subject has exposed wood that could lead to more damage, then this would be a soundness issue and the appraiser should make the report subject to repair.

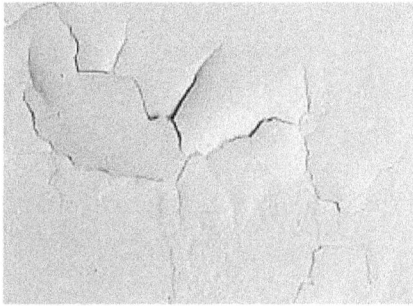
29

This looks wet. I would make this subject to repair. Let's take a look at another one:

[30] **As long as it is not wet, I would make a note in the report.**

---

[29] http://tallahasseehomeandwoodstainingexperts.com/blog/
[30] http://www.inspectapedia.com/PaintFailure/Paint_Mistakes_to_Avoid.htm

Moving on, let's look at minor plumbing leaks.

Minor plumbing leaks (such as leaky faucets). So, the bathroom faucet has a slight leak, no problem. Make a note and discuss the issue in the report.

31

Defective floor finish or covering (worn through the finish, badly soiled carpeting). The house has really nasty carpet and vinyl. Do I make it subject to? No. You will make a note and write about the issue in the report.

---

31 http://www.infomediu.eu/top-water-conservation-tips/

Evidence of previous (non-active) wood destroying Insect damage where there is no evidence of unrepaired structural damage. The house has previous termite damage that is non structural. This is not a problem for FHA. Make a note, take a photo and write about the issue in the report.

32

This seems fine to me. But, let's look at this one. It needs to be repaired.

33 **I would make this subject to repair.**

32 http://www.termiteforum.com/viewtopic.php?f=5&t=225

Rotten or worn out counter-tops.

If the subject has rotten or worn out counter-tops that do not present a danger to the residents, then you guessed it! Make a note, take a photo and discuss it in the report.

[34] This is not what I am talking about.

This countertop would need to be repaired or replaced as it is a safety and sanitary issue.

[33] http://www.servicemagic.com/rated.NationalProperty.14152108.html

[34] http://www.diychatroom.com/f49/unscheduled-kitchen-bath-remodel-dead-cat-mold-shoddy-work-many-pics-42441/

Chapter Five – Checklist Chapter

FHA Property Appraisal Inspection Checklist

The following items are required for appraisal inspection by the appraiser:

Interior Stuff	X
Turn on dishwasher and check for leaks.	
Flush toilet, check for leaks and check to see if water pressure drops on faucet after the flush	
1. Check kitchen and bathroom faucets for water pressure, also, check kitchen faucet for length of time until water changes from cold to hot. 2. Turn on shower and check for major leaks.	
Check windows throughout the house to make sure they are operational.	
Turn on range and oven to determine if they work.	
Turn on AC and determine if it blows cool air.	
Turn on heat and determine if it blows hot air. (In the summer, it may not be possible to turn heat on, make a note in the appraisal if this occurs.)	
Check at least one electrical outlet in each room. If you discover one that does not work, then check several more in the room.	
Turn on lights in each room, if you discover a problem, make a note and mention in the appraisal report. If you discover a safety issue, then make it subject to that item being checked by a professional.	
View the attic for previous fire, flood, etc. The requirement is to view the attic up to your chest.	
Exterior Stuff	**X**
View the crawl space for dampness, rodents, etc. The requirement is to view the crawl space up to your chest. FHA/HUD recommends a minimum of 18 inches for crawl space. If it is not 18 inches, then make a note with photo in the report.	
Observe the roof from the ground level. Use binoculars to obtain a better view of the roof. The roof must have a remaining economic life of 2 years or greater. Check for water stains inside the house for possible leaks. If it has a water stain, feel the stain, if wet then make a note with photos and the appraisal should be completed as repaired, (subject to the installation of a new roof).	
Observe the foundation and look for cracks and settlement. If there is evidence that the slab has failed, then make the appraisal subject to a satisfactory structural inspection. If the cracks and settlement are normal, then make a note in the report.	
Security Windows must have a quick release button, if not then make it subject to.	
Make a note of any UST's (Underground Storage Tank).	
If there is evidence of current infestation, then the appraisal should be completed subject to a termite inspection. If the evidence indicates previous damage, make a note with photos in the appraisal report.	
Lead Based Paint. So, you are appraising a house built prior to 1978 and the paint is peeling, cracking, etc. You make the appraisal subject to the paint issue being cured. Be sure to spell out the year built and why it is an issue.	
Photographs: Front/Side, Rear/Side, Street, interior always help.	
Unacceptable Locations: Environmental hazards, noxious odors, offensive sights or excessive noise. Contact the DE underwriter for directions on how to proceed.	
Grading/Drainage: If the topography appears to drain toward house (slab), the grading will be required to flow water away from house.	

FHA Property Appraisal Manufactured House Checklist

Manufactured Houses: Gather information from the HUD Data plate.	
Name and address of the plant.	
Serial number, model designation, and date built. (If the data plate is missing, you can make the appraisal subject to providing the information to the underwriter. This information can be obtained from www.ibts.org/label.	
Permanent Foundation (Need engineer's certification). The engineer's certification should be referenced in the appraisal report. A plastic skirt is allowed to be around the foundation; however, the actual foundation must be concrete, treated wood, etc.	
Towing and hitches must be removed.	
Must have utility connection.	
GLA must be at least 400 square feet.	
If any additions have been made, then another structural report will be required for safety compliance.	
Use 1004C form for these houses.	
You must use at least two manufactured houses as comparable sales.	
It must be taxed as real estate, not personal property.	
The house must be at or above the **flood level**. As the appraiser, you	

will report the flood area for the subject site; however, if you believe the subject is close to the flood area, you should indicate within the report.	
If you discover the subject has been moved more than once, then the house is ineligible for FHA financing. So, you will report what you discover.	
The cost approach is required for new construction manufactured houses. Additionally, the invoice should be attached to the appraisal report.	

Manufactured House

[35]

Look for the tag!

[35] http://www.harborheightshomes.com/forsale.asp

HUD (Red Tag)

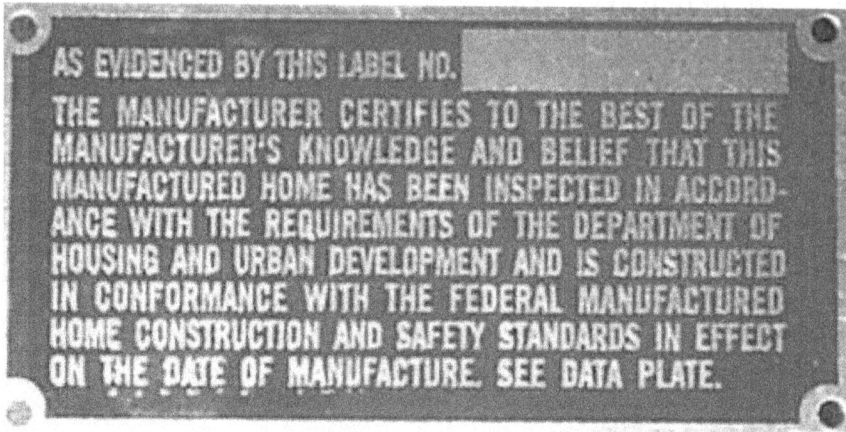

HUD Data Plate

You will need to locate this at the Manufactured house. It could be anywhere; however, please look under the kitchen sink, master bedroom closet or utility room.

FHA Property Appraisal Modular Checklist House

Appraise like a normal single family.	
Use modular house comparable sales.	
Take photos of the state tags, etc.	
Check with the DE underwriter for further clarification in your area.	
Make sure it is taxed as real estate.	

Modular house

36

---

[36] http://www.cabinstocottages.com/modular.htm

You will need to locate the state tag on a modular home as follows:

Modular housing is built to comply with North Carolina building codes. Modular homes are regulated by the Manufactured Building Division of the North Carolina Department of Insurance. The Department insures that the homes are built to the North Carolina State Uniform Residential Building Code. Because modular homes are built to the same code as stick-built homes, some believe that they can choose stick built homes as comparable sales for modular homes. This, however, is not always the case.

There are two types of modular homes: off-frame and on-frame. An off-frame house is built on a carrier, transported to a building site on the carrier, and then either craned or rolled onto a foundation. An on-frame modular home is built on a steel frame, towed to a job site, and then affixed to a foundation using the frame as part of the foundation. Both on-frame and off-frame modular homes are regulated by the Manufactured Building Division of the North Carolina Department of Insurance. Both types of modular homes have a silver label with red lettering, the seal of the State of North Carolina, and the words "State of North Carolina modular construction validating stamp." This Silver seal is usually located inside the home. Some manufacturers build the same floor plan with the same exterior elevations for both modular and manufactured homes. An appraiser can use the state modular seal and the HUD seal to verify whether a home is a modular home or a manufactured home.

Source: North Carolina Appraisal Board - Fall, 2002 Newsletter.

Now, let's review what is required for new construction.

FHA Property Appraisal New Construction Checklist

New Construction: **When do I need plans and specs?** Good question.

(Mortgagee Letter 2006-33)

Proposed Construction.	If the land is still dirt, then you need plans and specs. Thus, the house is considered to be proposed construction.
Under Construction.	If the house is started and is in process of being built, then it is a house that is under construction, then you still need plans.
Existing Construction.	However, if the house is 90% or more complete, then you do not need plans and specs. So, you would measure and inspect the house as normal. You will need to know what type of appliances and interior finish will be included.
Plans and Specs Requirements.	**What should be included in the plans and specifications?** Lender should provide a complete set of approved plans and specifications. These plans must include specifications. These specs should include the types of appliances, windows, building materials, etc. The plans should include an elevation drawing, floor-plan with measurements, and foundation detail.
Age of Subject Property.	If the house is less than 13 months old, then state the month and year built. Why? I have no idea, mainly because FHA asked us to do so.

FHA Property Appraisal Hazards Checklist

Stationary storage tanks containing flammable or explosive material.	
Flood hazard areas: If an area is known for flooding or if it is located within the 100 year flood area, this would need to be addressed by the appraiser.	
Smoke, fumes, offensive noise and odors: The appraiser should be watching for a. excessive smoke, b. fog, c. excessive dampness, d. poor surface drainage, e. stagnant ponds and marshes, f. noxious odors, g. chemical fumes.	
Overhead high-voltage transmission lines: The house is eligible for FHA financing if it is not located within the easement of these high voltage lines, etc.	
Proximity to high-pressure gas: this would include fast food restaurants (just kidding), seriously, it would include high pressure gas lines that are sometimes buried along the perimeter of a subdivision. These lines are usually marked with a warning sign. Be very careful with this hazard as their can be great danger of loss of life. If the subject improvements are located within 10 feet of the outer boundary, you will need to gain insight from the underwriter on how to complete the assignment.	
Special airport hazards: If the subject is located within the flight path now or in the future, the appraiser will need to comment on marketability.	
Airport noise and hazards: airport noise can be overwhelming if the houses are located too close to the airport runways. The general rule of thumb: if the subject is located within 5 miles of an airport, then the appraiser needs to comment on marketability of the subject property.	
Heavy Traffic: if a house is located too close to a highway or busy road this can lead to excessive noise from cars and trucks and lessen the economic life of a single family residence.	
Slush pits: Slushes from Sonic are good, but not the pits.	
Operating and abandoned oil or gas wells: The property will not be eligible for an FHA loan if it (improvements) is located within 300 feet of an active or planned drilling site. If an oil well exists, then the property would be ineligible if it is closer than 75 feet to the subject property improvements.	
Subsidence: this happens when the ground sinks. Properties that are located in areas of subsidence will not be eligible if the conditions threaten the health and safety of the occupants. When in doubt,	

Revisiting the FHA Appraisal, 1.0, 01/01/2011, JCJ, No Single or complete part of this workbook can be reprinted or duplicated in any way without the permission of Dr. J. Craig Julian, SRA, MRICS. If you have any questions regarding this material please e-mail craigjulian@gmail.com.

contact the underwriter and they will assist in your decision of whether to require a structural inspection.	
Topography: This is the lay of the land, it can be flat, hilly, mountainous, etc. These potential hazards should be carefully analyzed for marketability and value if the subject property connects with one of these property challenges. If you feel overwhelmed regarding these types of property hazards, you should consider an appraisal seminar to further your knowledge.	

One last time: HUD/FHA has three primary concerns in relation to property:

1. Correct physical deficiencies that affect the structural integrity.

2. Protect the security of the property.

3. Protect the health and safety of the occupants.

If a repair does not fit into one of these categories, then it should not be a repair on the appraisal report. Remember, the three S's from the introduction? They are Safety, Soundness and Security.

In regard to repairs, if an item has two years of economic life left, you will not require the item to be repaired. For example, if a roof is close to replacement, but you cannot determine if it has two years of economic life, you can recommend a roof inspection.

Challenge/Quiz

1. What are the three S's again?

2. What about well and septic again? In other words, what should I

   observe in regard to a water well and septic tank?

Now, let's determine what you learned by reviewing the final case studies of the course. They are located on the next few pages.

Chapter Six: Case Studies in FHA Appraisal

Now it is time to apply what you have learned through the application of case studies. So, please work through these and enjoy the learning process. Please answer and support your answers.

1. The subject property is located at 14001 Mallory Lane, Raleigh, NC. It contains 1,497 square feet and enjoys 3 bedrooms, 2 bathrooms and a 2 car garage. It was built by the Kellogg brothers in 1963. The lot size is 90 X 130 with a view of the woods.

Based on the photographs, would you make the appraisal report subject to or "as is"?

2. The subject property is located at 5618 Hialeah Street, Dallas, TX. It contains 2,398 square feet and enjoys 4 bedrooms, 3 bathrooms and a 3 car garage. It was built by the Grace Companies in 1980. The lot size is 5,000 square feet and has a view of the public golf course. The subject also has a large wood deck that measures 12 x 12.

Based on the photographs, would you make the appraisal report subject to or "as is"?

---

[37] http://www.diychatroom.com/f9/where-porch-roof-meets-wood-siding-41820/

3. The subject property is located on 2 acres and has a physical address of 8819 Potter Road, Indian Trail, NC. It contains 1,398 square feet and enjoys 3 bedrooms, 2 bathrooms and no garage. It was built by Fleetwood Homes in 1989. It has a water well and septic system.

38

Seriously, try this one:

39

a. Based on the photographs and above information, what factual information do you need to be able to complete the appraisal report? (Hint: Tag your it! And consumer reports best friend).

b. How many manufactured home comparables does FHA desire that you use in the sales comparison approach?

c. In regard to the foundation, what should you look for?

---

[38] http://www.emmitsburg.net/humor/archives/marriage/marriage_8.htm
[39] http://elizabethtown-pennsylvania.olx.com/charming-doublewide-mobile-home-for-sale-iid-13428740

4. The subject property is located on a 75 X 150 site and and has a physical address of 1009 Kirby Drive, Houston, TX. It contains 2,500 square feet and enjoys 4 bedrooms, 2.5 bathrooms and a 3 car garage. It was built by Slick Willy Homes in 1989. The majority of the subdivision has lots that measure 75 X 125. It has well and septic. The house is in good overall condition.

40

Would you make this report subject to?

---

[40] http://www.realpagessites.com/islandsepticsystems/sewage-septic-facility.html

5. The subject property is located on a 50 X 125 site and and has a physical address of 1919 Johnston Drive, Buffalo, NY. It contains 1,250 square feet and enjoys 2 bedrooms, 2 bathrooms and a 1 car garage. It was built by the Trump Companies in 1995. It has city well and sewer. The house is in average overall condition. There is evidence of previous termite damage on the rear of the house.

What should you do as the appraiser concerning the termite damage?

41

---

41 http://www.securitypest.com/termite-pictures-damage-photos.htm

6. The subject property is located on a 60 X 150 site and has a physical address of 10919 Hwy 75 East, San Diego, CA. It contains 1,001 square feet and enjoys 2 bedrooms, 1 bathrooms and a 1 car garage. It was built by the Sunshine Builders in 1965. It has city well and sewer. The house is in average overall condition.

What major issue should you be concerned with? (Hint: Highways are not kids best friends).

7. The subject property is located on an 8,500 square foot site and has a physical address of 1320 Wall Street, Midland, TX. It contains 2,101 square feet and enjoys 3 bedrooms, 2.5 bathrooms and a 2 car garage. It was built by Big Tex Builders in 1965. The roof is over 25 years old. It has city well and sewer. The house is in average overall condition.

Based on the photograph and age of the roof, what should you do as the appraiser?

42

---

[42] http://inspectapedia.com/roof/Worn_Out_Slate_Roofs.htm

8. The subject property is located on a 400 X 100 site and has a physical address of 1001 Sweet Grace Lane, Chicago, IL. It contains 1,922 square feet and enjoys 3 bedrooms, 2 bathrooms and a 2 car garage. It was built by Mario Brothers in 1965. The typical lot is 200 X 100. It has city well and sewer. The house is in average overall condition.

STREET

Based on the foregoing information, what should you do in regard to the appraisal?

Excess

Surplus

AVENUE

STREET

43

---

[43] http://www.e-rallc.com/Siteconcepts

9. The subject property is located on a 5 acre site and and has a physical address of 15 Kings Paradise. It contains 4,000 square feet and enjoys 5 bedrooms, 2 bathrooms and a 1.5 car garage. It was built by Country Bob Builders in 1995. It has city water and sewer. The house is in good overall condition.

Based on the foregoing information, what major issues due you suspect?

44

_____

[44] http://home.howstuffworks.com/home-improvement/construction/materials/rubber-roofs.htm/printable

10. The subject property is located on a 90 X 180 site and and has a physical address of 1002 Abbey Lane, Westfield, Ohio. It contains 2,001 square feet and enjoys 3 bedrooms, 2 bathrooms and a 2 car garage. It has city well and sewer. The house is proposed construction by Lennar Homes.

Based on the foregoing information, what items do you need as the appraiser before you can complete the appraisal assignment?

45

---

[45] http://tallahassee.olx.com/lake-talquin-vacant-lot-93-acre-with-360-lake-frontage-on-peninsula-iid-12070535

11. The subject property is located at 1201 Hialeah Street, Houston, TX. It contains 1,488 square feet and enjoys 3 bedrooms, 1 bathrooms and a 1 car garage. It was built by the Joseph and Company in 1963. The lot size is 90 X 130 with a view of the woods.

Based on the photographs, what would you do? Leave, Leave, Leave.......

46

46 http://www.trendir.com/house-design/farmhouse_homes/?start=10

Glossary

Major Forces that affect Real Estate:
Physical/environmental relates to the items such as climate, mountains, hills, beaches, rivers, streams, lakes, etc.
Economic activity relates to the economy that can be affected by interest rates, employment levels, terrorist attacks, developer participation, etc.
Governmental activity relates to taxation of real estate, federal reserve activity such as interest rate hikes, reserve requirements, and the purchasing of treasury bills.
Social relates to the expected norm of an area. For example if it is typical to have a sprinkler system, then most of the houses will have a sprinkler. The social force is more difficult to quantify due to the often unspoken words regarding the issue.

Real estate vs. real property: Real estate relates to the tangible items such as brick and mortar, roof, trees, landscaping, etc.

Real property vs. personal property: Real property relates to the right to use the real estate and other items associated with the property. For example, real property would be the right to use a golf course that is associated with a subdivision with golf course membership.

Fixtures: These are items that are generally attached to the subject property, For example, a toilet, kitchen cabinets, ceiling fans are all fixtures. Generally, fixtures are based on the three tests: a. How is the item attached?, b. Tradition or custom of the area, c. What was the intent of the person who attached item? For example, in most states a refrigerator is considered personal property, yet a range/oven is considered part of the real estate.

Trade fixtures: These items are associated with the tenant's business. For example, a restaurant may install booths and tables in leased space. When the lease is over, the tenant may remove these items without recourse.

Deed restrictions: Technically restrictions on a deed. For example, one type of restriction would be a prohibition of firing a gun on a property. Another type of deed restriction would be covenants, conditions and restrictions. In a typical subdivision, CC and R's are typically very restrictive. For example, if a homeowner has a desire to add a swing-set to a backyard, permission would be required from a committee. These rules would be included in the CC and R documents.

Leases: A lease is a contractual relationship between a property owner labeled landlord, (lessor) and a tenant or lessee. There are several types of leases: a. Gross lease: Tenant pays a fixed amount to a landlord. B. Net Lease: Tenant pays a fixed amount plus additional items such as insurance, real estate taxes. C. Percentage lease: Tenant pays a fixed amount plus a percentage of the retail sales to a landlord. D. Ground lease: The tenant pays a lease amount based on the land only. For example, a tenant leases 2 acres of land and pays rent based on the land and then builds a building that he uses or leases to others. This type of lease is typically a long term lease that is based on the economic life of a building.

Mortgages: A mortgage is a method of financing real estate. A mortgage is typically a two party instrument that includes a mortgagee (Lender) and mortgagor (borrower). The mortgage allows the borrower to receive funds to pay the seller for a property.

Easements: An easement is the right to use a property or part of a property for a period of time or indefinitely depending on what was negotiated between the parties involved. For example, a state department of transportation may purchase an easement across the landowner's property for a period of five years to store large equipment while a road is being increased in its width.

Liens: The old saying is "all mortgages are liens, but not all liens are mortgages". When a borrower signs a mortgage loan for a property this creates a lien against the property. When a lien is created against a property, it effects the borrowers ability to re-sale the property. Another type of lien is a material and mechanics lien. If an owner hires a contractor to build a wood deck and subsequently does not pay as noted in the contract, the contractor could file a material and mechanics lien. The owner would not be able to sell the property until the lien is paid. So, a lien is a restriction against a property.

Encroachments: When a neighboring property interrupts the subject property's enjoyment. For example, a neighbor builds a fence that overlaps the subject property's property line is an example of an encroachment.

Police power

Zoning: This is a land use restriction.

Building and fire codes

Environmental regulations: The federal and state government regulate the use of property in relation to the environment. Thus, if a business pollutes the ground water, the company will be required to clean up the land.

Taxation: The government has the right to tax to pay for operating expenses of its self.

Property tax: Taxes associated to a particular property.

Special assessments: This is a fee levied to pay for either a start up of a subdivision or a charge for something that is being added. For example, if a developer decides to add another swimming pool, they can pass this cost to the property owners.

Eminent domain: This is the government's right to take private property for the public good. Examples of eminent domain include land for a freeway system.

Escheat: If a person dies without a will and heirs, then the property is reverted back to the state.

Legal rights and interests

Fee simple estate: Fee simple, fee and fee simple absolute all are defined as complete ownership. Along with this ownership include the bundle of rights. These rights include the 1. right to build, 2. right to mortgage, 3. right to quiet enjoyment, 4. right to do nothing, 5. right to sell or lease a partial interest, 6. right to occupy.

Life estate: This is an interest that relates to the life of someone. For example, a grand mother can will her property to a grand son upon her death.

Leasehold interest: This is the interest of the tenant. For example, when a tenant signs a lease for 24 months for a property, they now have a leasehold interest in the property.

Leased fee interest: This is the interest of the owner. For example, when a person owns a house, then signs a lease for 24 months, they still own the property in fee, they have now given up the right to occupy.

Other legal interests

Easement: This is the right to use another owner's property for a period of time. For example, a state government needs a part of a property to store equipment for a period of time. They would need to purchase an easement for that part of the property. This would be a temporary easement. There are other types of easements such as an easement appurtenant. This type of easement is one that "runs with the land". So, if a person purchases a property with this type of easement, they would be able to sell the property with the easement. Another type of easement is an easement in gross. This type of easement is one that is tied to a person, not a property. So, when the person sells the property, they do not convey the easement.

Encroachment: This is when someone is in your space. For example, if an adjoining neighbor builds a fence and part of the fence lands on your property, this is an encroachment.

Forms of property ownership

Individual: This type of ownership is known as ownership in severalty. It can be one owner or one entity. The entity can be a small or large company.

Tenancies and undivided interests

Tenants in Common: A form of co-ownership by which each owner holds an undivided interest in real property as if he or she were sole owner. Each individual owner has the right to partition. Unlike joint tenants, tenants in common have no right of survivorship.

Joint Tenancy: Ownership of real estate between two or more parties who have been named in one conveyance as joint tenants. Upon the death of one joint tenant, his or her interest passes to the surviving joint tenant or tenants by the right of survivorship.

The difference between the two is the fact that under joint tenancy, the property passes to the other tenant. Thus, the last tenant standing under joint tenancy is the person that receives the property.

Special ownership forms

Condominiums: When someone purchases a condo, they have purchased air space in a particular unit and a prorata share of a HOA (Home Owners Association). The owner of the individual condo owns the airspace, but does not own the land underneath the unit. They have the right to use the complex facilities such as a swimming pool, tennis courts, etc.

Cooperatives: When you purchase a cooperative, you are purchasing shares of stock in a corporation. That corporation owns a building and the person that owns the stock receives a proprietary lease to a particular unit.

Timeshare: A timeshare is the right to use a property of a specific period of time.

Legal descriptions

Metes and bounds: This type of legal description is typically used in more rural areas. It is described based on minutes, distance and directions.

Government survey: This type of legal description is used to describe large tracts of land.

Lot and block: This type of legal description is related to a typical residential subdivision.

Transfer of title

Basic types of deeds: A deed transfers ownership from a seller to a buyer: (Grantor to grantee)

Warranty or General warranty deed: This type of deed provides a warranty from the sovereignty of the soil to the time of transfer. This type of deed provides the greatest type of protection.

Special warranty deed: This type of deed provides a warranty from the time when the property was purchased to the present time of transfer. This type of deed provides slightly less protection than the general warranty deed.

Quit claim deed: This type of deed provides no warranty at all. When someone sells using a quit claim deed, they are stating the following: "I am not guaranteeing anything. I do not own the property, but I will sell you what I have".

Recordation:
a. This is the recording of the deed. Deeds are typically recorded at the county clerk's office or court house.
b. They do not have to be recorded to be valid, but recording provides constructive notice.

Market value or value in exchange: This concept is what a typical buyer will pay for something. For example, if a stainless and gold Rolex sells for $15,000, this represents the market price. However, if 10 of these watches' sell for $10,000, then the market value is $10,000 for similar items.

Price: This is a fact. The price is what someone actually pays for something.

Cost: The cost is what it takes to produce something. For example, if it takes $2,000 + $3,000 + $3,000 equals $8,000. $8,000 is the cost to produce the object.

Investment value: This is the value to an individual investor. For example, if an individual investor requires the appraiser to use a specific capitalization rate that is different from the market rate, the resulting value is labeled investment value.

Value in use: This term relates to how the property is being used. For example, if a building has high ceilings that allows for cranes. The value to the property user would be higher than the value to a typical user.

Assessed value: This is the value assessed by an appraisal district or tax assessor's office for tax purposes. The value may be higher or lower than market value.

Insurable value: This is the value that is assessed for insurance purposes.

Going concern value: This value relates to a business enterprise. It relates more to the business than the real estate (bricks and sticks). Ralph Lauren, Honda, Volvo, McDonalds are all examples of items that have going concern value. People purchase items due to the fact that these companies have a certain reputation called going concern value. Enron had great value until investors determined that they had no real value. Thus, it does not have any going concern value.

Anticipation: This is the thought process of the buyers of property. For example when a couple is purchasing a house, they think of all of the enjoyment they will receive by owning the house. They picture their "family" living large in the house for several years, then making big money when they sell. In relation to a commercial investor, they simply anticipate how much profit they will receive monthly and in the end when they sell. Both of these examples relate to the anticipation of ownership in a property.

Balance: The idea of balance relates to numerous concepts. However, one example is a neighborhood which is defined as a group of complementary land uses. In this group called a neighborhood, there will be a balance of uses. These uses will include single-family residences, multi-family, office buildings, retail, recreational facilities, places of worship, etc. These will need to planned in balance for maximum number of interested buyers.

Another example of the principle of balance relates to when a builder plans and designs a subdivision. She will design the subdivision to accommodate as many buyers as possible. She will build a 2,000, 2,500, 2,750 and 3,000. This will allow for more buyers and hopefully more profit.

Change: Nothing stays the same. Real estate values can change over night. If a Volkswagen plant is decided on January 19, 2008 for a small town, then real estate values will likely change. This exhibits the principle of change.

Competition: All properties are affected by the principle of competition. If a developer plans a retail shopping center, then starts construction on the center, while a developer starts construction on a center across the street, the first developer will have competition.

Conformity: The principle of conformity is based on the concept that values are maximized when there are house that conform to each other in a subdivision. The developer will plan the houses to conform to each other. The concept is not that all houses will be exact duplicates, but will complement each other.

Contribution: The principle of contribution represents the return on the investment made on a particular item. For example, if a homeowner replaces the Formica countertop with a Granite countertop, the contribution to the house is the incremental difference in value after the item was added.

Increasing and decreasing returns: This principle exhibits the fact that bigger is not necessarily better. If you have a 3,000 square foot house among other 3,000 square foot houses, but then you decide to add an additional 3,000 for a total of 6,000 square feet. You may not recapture the money spent on the additional 3,000 square feet. This concept of decreasing returns relates to the fact that people generally pay for what they need. Increasing returns is the antithesis of decreasing returns. If you have a 1,000 square foot house among 2,000 square foot houses, you may need to add an additional 1,000 square feet to conform to the subdivision. If the increase in value is equal or greater than the cost to add the additional 1,000 square feet, then the result is increasing return.

Opportunity cost: The concept of opportunity cost is based on what a prudent investor should have purchased. If you purchase an office building that produces a return of 12%, yet you turned down an investment opportunity to purchase a retail shopping center that produces an 18% return with the same risk, the opportunity cost is 6%.

Substitution: This concept is based on the fact that a prudent purchase will not pay any more than the cost to acquire an equally desirable property. The principle of substitution relates to all three approaches to value. In relation to the sales comparison approach, if the sales indicate a value opinion of $135,000 based on recent comparable sales, yet you can acquire a substitute property for $115,000, then the value would be $115,000.

Supply and demand: Supply is the amount of items for sell of a given product. Demand is the actual desire of the market for a given item. If demand remains the same and supply increase, then values will decline. If demand increases and supply increases, then value will be stable. If demand increases and supply decreases, then value will increase.

Surplus productivity: This is what is numerically left over after paying for land, labor capital and coordination.

Changes in supply vs. demand: Supply is the amount of items for sell of a given product. Demand is the actual desire of the market for a given item. If demand remains the same and supply increase, then values will decline. If demand increases and supply increases, then value will be stable. If demand increases and supply decreases, then value will increase.

Immobility of real estate: You cannot move real estate, therefore, it is immobile.

Segmented markets: The market can further segmented into sub-markets. These elements include: income, age, household size and lifestyle choices.

Regulations: Real estate is regulated from a national, state and local government.

Absorption analysis: This is an analysis of a particular market. This analysis will estimate how long it will take in the number of months to sell. For example, if there are 12 houses listed for sale and 12 sold last year, then the absorption rate is 1 per month.

Demographic data: This data will help an analyst understand who is living in the neighborhood. It will also assist the analyst in understanding who the potential buyer's would be.

Competition: All properties are affected by the principle of competition. If a developer plans a retail shopping center, then starts construction on the center, while a developer starts construction on a center across the street, the first developer will have competition.

Absorption: This is an analysis of a particular market. This analysis will estimate how long it will take in number of months to sell. For example, if there are 120 houses listed for sale and 120 sold last year, then the absorption rate is 10 house sales per month.

Forecasts: This concept is based on predicting the future based on current statistical information.

Existing space inventory: This term is an analysis of the space that is currently on the market for rent. For example, in regard to office space in a downtown area, the analyst would determine how much space is available in a downtown area.

Current and projected space surplus: This is the amount of space available and the projected space that will not be absorbed based on projections.

New space: This is simply the space that was recently completed and available for a new tenant.

Role of money and capital markets

Competing investments: There are always competing investments. But what is a competing investment? A competing investment is an alternative to the subject property. For example, if an analyst is evaluating a house, the competing investments would include the stock market, gold and silver, coins, as well as other real estate properties.

Sources of capital: These include banks, mortgage companies, pension funds, etc.

Real estate financing

Mortgage terms and concepts

Mortgagor: This term is defined as the borrower on a loan. If there are two borrowers, then they are termed co-mortgagors.

Mortgagee: This is the lender on a mortgage loan.

Principal and interest: The principal is the loan being paid back. This is the amount that was borrowed. The interest is the charge for using the money of the lender.

Mortgage payment plans

Fixed rate, level payment: Fixed simply means that the interest rate will not change over the life of the loan. Level payment simply means that the payment will not change over time.

Adjustable rate: An adjustable rate will adjust based on an index. This index could be a cost of savings index, consumer price index, Treasury bill index, etc.

Buydown: A buydown is the process of paying money to receive a lower interest rate on a mortgage loan.

Other

Types of mortgages

Conventional: A conventional loan is a mortgage loan that is not FHA and not VA.

Insured: FHA (Federal Housing Administration) insures mortgage loans.

Guaranteed: VA (Veterans Administration) guarantees mortgage loans for veterans.

Site description

Utilities: These include gas, water, electricity, and cable television.

Access: This term relates to ingress and egress of the property. This is how you enter the property.

Topography: This is the lay of the land. It can be flat like most of Texas, or hilly, mountainous or a combination of all three.

Size: This is the size of the site in terms of square footage or acreage. In regard to the size of the improvements, GLA (gross living area) is the amount of living area located above grade.

Improvement description

Size: This is the size of the site in terms of square footage or acreage. In regard to the size of the improvements, GLA (gross living area) is the amount of living area located above grade.

Acre of land: An acre of land contains 43,560 square feet. If the tract is square, then the tract of land is about 208.11 X 208.11.

Lineal Feet in a mile: There are 5,280 feet in a mile.

Number of acres in a section: A section of land is 1 mile square. Thus, 1 mile x 1 mile or 5,280 X 5,280 = 27,878,400 square feet. To convert to acres, simply divide the number of square feet of 27,878,400 by 43,560 (number of square feet in an acre) = 640 acres.

Condition: This term relates to the physical condition of the property. These items can be short lived and long lived items.

Utility: This is the how the property is being used. For example, if a house is 3,500 square feet and contains 2 bedrooms and the typical house contains 4 bedrooms, then the subject would have diminished utility.

Basic construction and design

Techniques and materials: These items include roofing materials such as composition, wood, metal, ceramic tile, hardie plank, etc. Exterior siding includes brick, wood siding, hardie plank, stucco, etc.

Foundations: This is the part of the structure that hold the improvements together. It is the bottom portion of the structure. Foundations can be basement, concrete slab or pier and beam.

Framing: This is the part of the improvements that holds the structure together. It can be made of steel or wood.

Finish (exterior and interior: These items include roofing materials such as composition, wood, metal, ceramic tile, hardie plank, etc. Exterior siding includes brick, wood siding, hardie plank, stucco, etc. Interior items include flooring: wood, ceramic tile, carpet, vinyl, etc.

Mechanical: This consists of heating and cooling, appliances, light fixtures, etc.

Functional utility: This term relates to the usability of the improvements. For example, if the subject is a house and contains functional issues in the floor plan such as the lack of a bathroom on the first floor in a two story house.

Four tests of Highest and Best Use

Physically possible: What can the subject land site be used for from a physical perspective? What improvement can physically fit on the subject site?

Legally permitted: This term relates to zoning or deed restrictions. What improvements can legally be placed on the land?

Economically feasible: What are the financial possibilities that will fit on the subject site? There may be several possibilities that will fit, for example, a medical center, pharmacy, etc.

Maximally productive: This term is the best and the most profitable improvements that will fit on the subject site.

Vacant site or as if vacant: This is the value of the land assuming its highest and best use.

As improved: This is the value of the improvements and the land as one unit.

Interim use: A property may be in process of changing to another highest and best use. For example, if the land is valued at $400,000 and the land and improvements are valued at $375,000, yet the cost of demolition exceeds $25,000, then the highest and best use is an interim use.

Compound interest concepts: The concept is that money can worth more today if you receive it today due to the fact that inflation can erase potential profit over time due to rising prices.

Future value of $1.00: This is very similar to a savings account. You invest money now and receive more money in the future. You earn interest on the principal as well as interest on the interest. For example, if you want to know how much money you will accumulate at the end of 5 years after saving $100 per month at 8%. You will use the following steps on the HP12C calculator.

Step 1: $100 CHS PMT (This tells the calculator how much you are investing monthly).

Step 2: 8 g i (This tells the calculator the interest rate to use for the calculation of the interest, you are using the g to convert it to monthly).

Step 2: 5 g n (This tells the calculator the length of the time to calculate the total).

Step 3: You press the FV (This stands for future value which calculates the total amount that will be available at the end of the period). $7,347.69 (This represents principal and interest. The total principal invested is $100 X 60 (5 years) equals $6,000, thus, the interest portion is $1,347.69).

Present value of $1.00: This concept is based on the fact that an investor desires a certain dollar amount at the end of a time period. For example, if you desire to have $10,000 in 5 years based on an interest rate of 7%. You will use the following steps on the HP12C calculator.

Step 1: $10,000 FV (This tells the calculator how much you desire to have).

Step 2: 7 i (This tells the calculator the interest rate to use for the calculation of the interest).

Step 2: 5 n (This tells the calculator the length of the time to calculate the total).

Step 3: You press the PV (This stands for present value which calculates the total amount that must be invested to have $10,000 in five years earning 7% interest). The PV of $10,000 assuming 7% and 5 years holding period is $7,129.86.

Future value of an annuity of $1.00 per period: This is very similar to an annuity purchased from a life insurance company. This concept will show the investor how much their investment will grow over time with periodic investments. So, if you invest $1,000 per year, earn 10% interest and do this for 4 years, how much money will you accumulate?

You will use the following steps on the HP12C calculator.

Step 1: $1000 CHS PMT (This tells the calculator how much you are investing yearly).

Step 2: 10 i (This tells the calculator the interest rate to use for the calculation of the interest, note: you are not using g since it is not a monthly investment).

Step 2: 4 n (This tells the calculator the length of the time to calculate the total).

Step 3: You press the FV (This stands for future value which calculates the total amount that will be available at the end of the period). $4,641 (This represents principal and interest. The total principal invested is $1000 X 4 years) equals $4,000, thus the interest represents $641).

Present value of an annuity of $1.00 per period: This is very similar to an annuity purchased from a life insurance company. This concept will demonstrate how much money, in a single payment, must be invested today and compounded into the future to equal a series of periodic payments in the future. So, if you have an investment opportunity to receive $2,000 a year for the next 5 years and you desire a return of 14% per year, how much can you afford to spend for this investment?

You will use the following steps on the HP12C calculator.

Step 1: $2,000 CHS PMT (This tells the calculator how much you are investing yearly).

Step 2: 14 i (This tells the calculator the interest rate to use for the calculation of the interest, note: you are not using g since it is not a monthly investment).

Step 2: 5 n (This tells the calculator the length of the time to calculate the total).

Step 3: You press the PV (This stands for present value which calculates the total amount that can be invested if they desire a 14% return and will receive $2,000 per year. The answer is $6,866.16.

Sinking fund factor: A sinking fund factor is used as a "rainy day account". The idea is that you will need money in the future to cover an expense in the future. Thus, you own an apartment complex and will need to replace all of the appliances in all 50 units in 12 years. The cost to replace all of these appliances is $100,000. How much money will need to be invested monthly assuming an interest rate of 6%?

You will use the following steps on the HP12C calculator.

Step 1: $100,000 FV (Future Value: This tells the calculator how much you will need for the appliances).

Step 2: 6 g i (This tells the calculator the interest rate to use for the calculation of the interest, note: you using g since you are saving monthly).

Step 2: 12 g n (This tells the calculator the length of the time to calculate the total, note: you using g since you are saving monthly).

Step 3: You press the PMT (This stands for payment which calculates the monthly payment of $475.85.

Installment **to amortize $1.00 (loan constant):** This is the amortization of a loan. The word amort means to kill off, thus when you make a payment, you are killing off your loan. So, if you desire to find the payment on a 15 year loan, with an interest rate of 5.5% and a sales price of $3,000,000 and a 80% LTV (loan to value ratio). What is the monthly payment?

You will use the following steps on the HP12C calculator.

Step 1: $2,400,000 PV (Present Value: This tells the calculator how much you are going to borrow).

Step 2: 5.5 g i (This tells the calculator the interest rate to use for the calculation of the interest, note: you using g since you are saving monthly).

Step 2: 15 g n (This tells the calculator the length of the time to calculate the total, note: you using g since you are saving monthly).

Step 3: You press the PMT (This stands for payment which calculates the monthly payment of $19,610.

Statistical concepts used in appraisal

Mean: This is the same as the average. To derive the mean, you add the numbers together and divide by the number in the set. Thus, 75 + 100 + 102 + 104 + 106 + 200 equals 687. Then, you divide the 687 by the number in the set, thus, 687 / 6 = 114.50 or 115. This is typically not the best indicator of an accurate number. Related to this concept is a weighted average.

 Weighted Average: A weighted average is a weighting of numbers within a set. This can be utilized for a sales comparison analysis as follows. For example, in a scenario of comparable sales that require many adjustments due to the diverse physical characteristics in a neighborhood, a weighted average may be the best method of determining a value opinion. Sale 1 has an adjusted value of $226,000 and you believe it is 25% comparable to the subject ($56,500). Sale 2 has an adjusted value of $245,000 and you believe it is 45% comparable to the subject ($110,250). Sale 3 has an adjusted value of $265,000 and you believe it is 20% comparable to the subject ($53,000). Sale 4 has an adjusted value of $210,000 and you believe it is 10% comparable to the subject ($21,000. Then you would simply apply the math by adding the amounts indicated by each comparable sale. $56,500 + $110,250 + $53,000 + $21,000 equals $240,750. This method requires judgment and actual reconciliation, unlike the mean/average method which requires no judgment. In this case the average of the set is $236,500 which is $5,000 different than the weighted average.

Median: The median is the middle number in a set of numbers. If the set includes an odd amount of numbers in the set, you select the middle number. If the numbers in the set are eve, then you select the middle two numbers and divide by two.

Thus, 75, 100, 102, 104,106, and 200. You add 102 + 104 which equals 206 and divide by 2 and that equals 103. If you contrast the average/mean which indicated 114.50 or 115 which does not really represent the set with the indicated median of 103 which does represent the set. Note: if a number appears twice in a set, you include it twice.

Mode: The mode is the number that occurs the most times in a set. For example, if you have the following set of numbers: 100, 100, 102, 103, 106, 108, 110, 110, 110, and 118. The mode is 110 due to the fact that it occurs the most times in the set.

Range: In a set of numbers, the range is the difference between the highest number and the lowest number. So, if you have the following set of numbers: 100, 102, 110, 112. The range is 12.

Research and selection of comparable sales

Data sources: Public and private. These include MLS (Multiple Listing Service), tax records, county deed records, etc.

Verification: Verification of data can be verbal, electronic paper copy or an exterior drive by of the property.

Units of comparison: Properties can be compared based on many different units; however, some of the more common include: gross living area, garage, site size, etc.

Income

Potential gross income multiplier: Sales Price divided by the potential gross income equals PGIM.

Effective gross income multiplier: Sales price divided by the effective gross income (potential gross income minus vacancy and collection losses) equals EGIM.

Overall rate or Overall Capitalization Rate: This is the overall rate for the property. For example, to determine the overall rate, you would divide the net income by the value or sales price. The result is an overall cap rate.

Size:

Square foot or GLA (Gross Living Area)

Acres: 43,560 square feet in a acre of land.

Frontage: Golf Course, Lake, Mountain, etc.

Utility (examples only): Rooms, Bedrooms, Baths, and Living Units (for 2-4 family properties).

Elements of comparison:

Property rights conveyed: What rights were conveyed with the transfer? Fee Simple, Leased fee/Leasehold, Easements and airspace.

Easements: An easement is a right to use land for a particular portion of land. An easement can affect the resale due to the limitation imposed by the easement.

Leased fee/Leasehold: Fee simple is complete ownership. So, you purchase in fee, then sign a lease with a tenant, you now have a leased fee estate and the tenant has a leasehold estate.

Subsurface and Mineral rights: These are rights than can be transferred.

Others

Financing terms and cash equivalency

Loan payment: This can include principal and interest or principal, interest, taxes and insurance.

Loan balance: The loan balance is amount borrowed after the down payment or equity payment.

Conditions of sale

Arm's length sale: This assumes that the parties are not related in any way. For example, if one of the buyer's works for the seller's husband, this would violate the principle of an arm's length transaction. Please note that a non-arms length transaction does not mean the sales price is inflated, it simply is an alert to the analyst.

Personalty: This is personal property and should be valued separately if part of the appraisal assignment.

Market conditions at time of contract and closing: The analyst should determine if the market has increased since the date of sale for each comparable.

Location: This relates to the physical site of the subject property and the comparable sales.

Physical characteristics: These include GLA (Gross Living Area), Garage, Amenities: Pool, Spa, Tennis Courts, Guest House.

Tenant improvements

Adjustment process

Sequence of adjustments:
Property Rights Conveyed
Financing Terms
Conditions of Sale
Market Conditions
Location
Physical Characteristics

Dollar adjustments: These can be made for any item that is different between the comparable and the subject property.

Percentage adjustments: These can be applied when the market recognizes in this manner. For example, if one of the comparable sales is 10% superior to the subject, then you would deduct 10% from the sale.

Paired sales analysis: This method entails locating comparable sales that are very comparable to each with minor differences between them. For example, if sale A has a sales price of $250,000 with an interior location and sale B has a sales price of $350,000 located on a lake. The houses are very comparable to each other with the exception of the lake. Then the adjustment for lake is $100,000.

Survey Method: This method entails surveying the neighborhood to assist with adjustments in the sales comparison approach. For example, an appraiser could develop a questionnaire regarding buyer's reaction to a swimming pool. So, she could ask 1. Would you pay more for a house with a swimming pool than one without? 2. How much would you pay for a swimming pool with spa? a. waterfall?, b. diving board etc. This method can also be very beneficial when the subject property has a particular issue such as mold, cracked slab, toxic waste, etc. Another version of the survey method is to contact other appraisers/agents active in your market and ask their opinion regarding the problem you are attempting to solve.

Cost Contributory Method: This method entails determining the cost of a particular item, then you deduct the depreciation (Physical, Functional and External) the remaining portion is the adjustment.

Application of sales comparison approach

The basic premise of the sales comparison approach is as follows: substitute or like properties are compared to a subject property (the one being appraised). These substitute properties are labeled comparable sales. The comparable sales have the following characteristics: sold recently, located nearby, are similar in regard to physical attributes, etc. The sales comparison is based on the principle of substitution. The principle of substitution states that a prudent buyer would purchase the least expensive property among equals. Therefore, if you have two properties with equal attributes, the prudent purchaser would buy the one with the lowest sales price.

The mechanics of the sales comparison approach are comparing substitute properties to the subject property. If the comparable sale is superior to the subject, then the appraiser will subtract. On the contrary, if the comparable sale is inferior, then the appraiser will add. These additions and subtractions are designed to make the comparable sale equal with the subject property to lead to an opinion of value. Further, the additions and subtractions are labeled adjustments. There has been great debate about the adjustment process. The most proven way to derive adjustments is labeled matched pairs analysis.

Paired Data Analysis or Matched Pairs analysis is the most accepted process of deriving adjustments. The basic process consists of analyzing two sales with one major difference. For example, sale one is located at 5618 Nightmare on Elm contains 2,700 square feet and sold for $267,000, and sale two is located at 5617 Kruger Special contains 2,500 square feet and sold for $260,000. The only difference between sale one and sale two is the difference in livable area of 200 square feet and a difference in sales price of $7,000. This indicates a price per square foot of $35. The method is to review the difference in livable area which in this case is 200 square feet and divide into the difference in sales price of the comparable sales which is $7000. Thus $7000 / 200 = $35 per square foot.

Land value Methods

Sales comparison: This approach entails locating comparable properties that have recently sold, then comparing those properties to the subject property, making appropriate adjustments and deriving a value opinion of the lot or land. For example, you locate three properties that are very similar to the subject that sold for $100,000, $120,000 and $130,000. After making adjustments, the range is narrowed to $110,000 to $120,000. The subject site is worth $110,000 to $120,000. The final reconciliation would be based on which comparable sale is most similar to the subject property.

Land residual: There are three steps to the land residual method of valuing sites.

Step 1: Determine the contributory value of the improvements:

Develop the opinion of value for the improvements. b. Then allocate the net income attributable to the improvements.

Step 2: Determine the Net Income Attributable to the land:
Subtract the income to the improvements from the total net income.
The resulting net income is attributable to the land.

Step 3: Determine the Land Value
Apply the direct capitalization approach to the land value.
The capitalization rate should be market driven.

Sample Problem: An office building is being valued. The building is valued at $500,000. Net income is $50,000, with 75% being attributable to the building. The market driven capitalization rate is 9%. What is the indicated land value via Land Residual Method?

$50,000 x .75% = $37,500 (NOI to the building).
$50,000 - $37,500 = $12,500 NOI to the land).
$12,500 / 9% (.09) = $138,888.89 (Indicated value of the land via Land Residual)

Allocation: The allocation method is based on historical ratios of land to building ratio for an area. There are three steps in the process of determining applicable land value ratios.

Step 1: Identify Comparable Data
Locate unimproved sites known as lot sales
Locate improved sales in the same area as the lot sales.

Step 2: Identify the ratio of land value to improved value
Divide the land value by the improved value.

Step 3: Apply the indicated ratio to the subject property for a land value opinion.

For example, you locate the following information to derive allocation ratios.

Sale Number	Improved Sale	Unimproved Sale	Indicated Ratio
1	$800,000	$200,000	25%
2	$750,000	$225,000	30%
3	$1,000,000	$300,000	30%
4	$900,000	$250,000	27.7%

Thus, if the subject is valued at $875,000, a reasonable land value opinion would be (25%) $218,750 to (30%) $262,500.

Extraction: The process of extraction extracts or separates the land value out of the total sales price. This method can work in older houses as well as newer houses.

Step 1: Locate comparable sales within the subject area for consideration.
Step 2: Calculate the replacement cost for the comparable sales.
Step 3: In the case of new construction, subtract the replacement cost new from the sales price of the comparable sale.
Step 4: The result is the indicated land value.

For example, you have located the following sales:

Sale Number	Sales Price	RCN	Indicated Land Value	Indicated PSF
1: 20,000 SF	$500,000	$400,000	$100,000	$5.00
2: 25,000 SF	$600,000	$495,000	$105,000	$4.20
3: 22,500 SF	$550,000	$445,000	$105,000	$4.67
4: 25,000	$575,000	$465,000	$110,000	$4.40

The indicated value per square foot is $4.20 to $5.00. Thus, the value of the subject site will be within the range.

Plottage and assemblage

Plottage is the combining of lots to create a higher value. For example, if you own a lot that measures 50'X 100' that could contain a house with 1,500 square feet of GLA and is valued at $100,000. However, if you combine the subject lot with the adjoining lot that also measures 50' x 100', thus allowing for a house with 3,000 to 4,000 square feet of GLA. The result is a large site that is worth $250,000 due to its increased utility.

Assemblage is the combining of lots to create greater utility for the subject. For example, if the subject contains a site that measures 25' x 100' that could not contain a house due to its small size with a value of $15,000. However, if you combined the subject lot with another site that measures 25' x 100', the result would be an increased utility and a value of $30,000.

Reproduction vs. replacement cost:

Reproduction Cost: This is the cost to reproduce the subject exactly as it stands. As improvements age, it is increasing difficult to estimate the reproduction cost for the property.

Replacement cost: This is the cost to replace the improvements. It is known as replication. It is usually based on a national cost service such as Marshall and Swift. When using this type of cost, functional inadequacies is eliminated due to the fact that the analyst is replicating not reproducing the improvements. However, functional super-adequacies are not eliminated.

Comparative unit method: This method is also called the cost comparable method. For example, if the analyst is evaluating a 2,000 square foot basic tract built house that sold for $100 per square foot based on improvement value. She can apply the $100 to the subject house as a cost comparable with further support from a cost service.

Unit-in-place method: This method estimates the cost of construction by adding all of the major component parts of a structure. These components include the roof, framing, HVAC, etc.

Quantity survey method: This method specifies the quantity of each part or material used to build a structure. Note: This method is not commonly used in appraisal.

Cost service index: The cost index method estimates the cost based on its original cost and multiplying it by an index factor based on how long ago it was constructed. For example, the original structure cost $1,000,000 in 1988. However, the current index is 1.5, thus, $1,000,000 x 1.5 = $1,500,000 construction cost.

Accrued depreciation: This is the total amount of depreciation that has occurred since the improvements were built. This depreciation is from all three types: Physical Functional and external.

Types of depreciation

Physical deterioration: This is the actual wear and tear due to elements or other forces. It can be peeling paint, rotted wood, etc.

Curable: **Incurable**: This is determined by the return on investment. For example, if the item will cost $1,000 and the return is $900, then it is not curable, it is incurable. If the item cost $1,000 and the return is $1,500, the it is curable. However, another factor is how much damage will be done if the work is not completed. A third factor is what happens if the work is not completed in regard to marketing time. Will the marketing time be increased if the work is not completed?

Short-lived: These are items that can be replaced. These items include: Carpet, HVAC system, Interior and Exterior Paint.

Long-lived: These are items that generally cannot be replaced. These items include: Foundation, framing and insulation.

Functional obsolescence: This is a loss in value due to a super adequacy or inadequacy. Functional obsolescence is generally inside the property boundaries. The market place is the measuring stick for whether an item is curable or incurable.

Curable: **Incurable**: If a house has no central air conditioning and the cost to add is $5,000 and the return is $5,000 or greater, then it is considered to be curable. If it does not add $5,000, then it is considered to be incurable.

External obsolescence: This is a loss in value due to something located outside of the property boundaries. This type of obsolescence is generally not curable; however, sometimes it is cured by the market place.

Locational: This is a loss in value due to the fact that it is located near something undesirable. This can be a house that is located near a rail road tracks, highway, shopping center, landfill, etc.

Economic: This is a loss in value due to the fact that something happened in the market place such as a recession, earth quake, hurricane, increase in interest rates, tight loan policy, etc.

Methods of estimating depreciation

Economic Age-life method: The formula for the age-life method is the effective age divided by the total economic life equals total accrued depreciation.

Breakdown method and sequence of
Deductions: This is also known as the modified economic age life breakdown method. The formula for this method is very similar to the economic age method with the exception that the deferred maintenance/physical curable items are deducted before the formula is being applied.

Market extraction of depreciation: This is similar to the extraction method for land value purposes. The formula is as follows: Sales price minus land value equals contributory value. Then the cost of the improvements is deducted from the contributory value. The difference is the accrued depreciation.

Application of the cost approach:

Cost Approach Formula

The formula for the cost approach is Replacement cost new - depreciation + Land Value = Cost Approach to value.

Depreciation Formulas

Economic Age Life Method

Effective Age / Total Economic Life = Accrued Depreciation

For example, if the effective age is 20 years and the total economic life is 60 years, then the appraiser simply divides 20 / 60 years = 33 Percent accrued depreciation.

Another acceptable method is modified economic age life breakdown method. This method subtracts the deferred maintenance before estimating the effective age of the subject. Therefore, the effective age is completed after repairing the deferred maintenance. If the total depreciation is desired, then the incurable depreciation will need to be added to the curable. Thus, the formula is as follows:

Cost New - Curable (Deferred Maintenance) Effective age / Total Economic Life = Incurable Depreciation

Effective Age is not the actual or chronological age. It is a description of how old the subject appears to be. The effective age is based on appearance of the subject property. If the subject has been updated, then the effective age is lower than the actual age. If the subject has deferred maintenance, then the effective age is higher than the actual age. The formula is total economic life minus the remaining economic life equals the effective age. Although most people give an opinion of effective age based on the present condition of the improvements along with the consideration of functional utility and economic conditions.

Total Economic Life is the economic life of the property. This number represents how long the improvements will contribute to the overall value of the property. As noted in Highest and Best Use, when the as vacant value is higher than the as improved value, then subject improvements no longer represent the highest and best use and should be demolished. The formula is effective age plus the remaining economic life equals the total life. One method to assist the appraiser is to analyze properties in a similar market and determine their total economic life is before being torn down and a new improvement is built.

Remaining Economic Life is the life that remains at the time of appraisal from an economic prospective. Mathematically this number is the difference between the effective age and the total economic life. The formula is the total life minus the effective age equals the remaining economic life.

Estimation of income and expenses

Gross market income: This is the same as potential gross income. This is the income from all potential sources. **Market rent**: This is the rent that the tenant should be paying. It is based on what other properties are receiving in rent. **Contract rent**: This is what the tenant is contractually obligated to pay.

Effective gross income: (EGI) The formula for EGI is (PGI) Potential Gross Income minus vacancy and collection loss.

Vacancy: This is when tenants do not occupy the property. For example, if there are 100 units in the subject complex and 95 are occupied with paying tenants, then the property is 5% vacant and 95% occupied.

Collection loss: These are losses based on unpaid rent or bad checks.

Operating expenses

Fixed expenses: These are ongoing expenses that do not fluctuate with occupancy. In other words, they must be paid regardless of whether there are any tenants at all.

Variable expenses: These are expenses that vary with occupancy. They include maintenance and utilities.

Reserve for replacements: This is money that is set aside for expenses in the future. They include parts of the improvements that wear out over time. They include roofs, kitchen appliances, heating and air conditioning units, etc.

Net operating income: (NOI) The formula is Potential Gross Income minus vacancy and collection loss equals Effective Gross Income. Then Effective Gross Income minus operating expenses equals Net Operating Income.

Gross rent multiplier (GRM) This term was once labeled gross monthly rent multiplier. The formula for GRM is sales price divided by the gross monthly rent. For example, if the sales price is $100,000 and the gross monthly rent is $1000, then $100,000 / $1,000 equals 100 (GRM). This indicates that it will take 100 months to receive your money back on the original sales price in gross dollars.

Gross rent multiplier analysis: The GRM can be utilized to derive adjustments in the sales comparison approach. For example, if a house backs to a busy highway and rents for $100 less than other houses in the area and the indicated GRM for the area is 100, then the loss in rent can be capitalized at $100 X 100 = $10,000 loss in value due to this location problem.

Direct capitalization: This is the method of calculating a single year's income divided by the capitalization rate equals a value via income capitalization approach.

Relevance and limitations: This method is utilized for commercial income properties as well as apartments, hotels, etc.

Overall capitalization rate: This is calculated by dividing the NOI by the sales price equals the overall capitalization rate. It is the capitalization rate for the land and improvements combined.

Gross income multiplier: (GIM): The formula for the GIM is sales price divided by the gross annual income. For example, if the sales price is $1,000,000 and the gross annual income is $100,000, then the GIM is 10. This indicated that it will take 10 years to receive the money back on the original sales price in gross dollars.

Net income ratio: The formula for the NIR is NOI (Net Operating Income divided by the EGI (Effective Gross Income).

Band of investment (mortgage equity) techniques: This method is utilized when there is a lack of capitalization rates available in the market place due to the lack of sales. It combines the mortgage constant and the required return on the equity or down payment.

There are a number of formulas/concepts that are quite simple that tend to assist the appraiser on the state exam. The following formulas and definitions are for your assistance.

Gross Market Income: PGI = Potential Gross Income: This is income from all potential sources. In regard to an apartment project, this income would include rent from apartments, rent from covered parking, and income from a washateria on site.

EGI: Effective Gross Income: The formula is PGI minus vacancy and collection loss equals EGI. Thus, if the potential gross income is $100,000 and the vacancy rate is 5%, and the collection loss is 5%. Then, $100,000 less 5% or $5,000 for vacancy and 5% or $5,000 for collection loss equals $90,000 EGI. Vacancy is the antithesis of occupancy. When an occupancy rate is discussed, this number represents how many people are actually occupying the property. Therefore, vacancy is when people are not occupying the property. Collection loss is the amount of money that is left unpaid by tenants. It can also occur when a tenant writes a check that is insufficient in regard to funds available.

The next step is to determine NOI: Net Operating Income. NOI is EGI minus operating expenses. Operating expenses are those expenses that are required to operate the property. These expenses include Fixed expenses: These expenses do not fluctuate with occupancy. These include real estate property taxes and insurance, Variable expenses are those that vary with occupancy. These items include leasing fees, management charges, utilities, general payroll, cleaning, maintenance, decorating, and supplies. The calculation of EGI minus operating expenses equal NOI.

How do I derive NOI again?

PGI	a. EGI	= NOI
Potential Gross Income	Effective Gross Income	Net Operating Income
Potential Income from all sources.	PGI – Vacancy and Credit/Collection Loss = EGI	EGI – Operating Expenses
Example - $150,000 PGI	PGI $150,000 - $15,000 (Vacancy and Collection Loss of 10%) = $135,000 EGI	EGI $135,000 - $35,000 (Operating Expenses) = $100,000 NOI.

Now that I am an expert on NOI, How do I derive the Capitalization Rate?

The formula is Net Operating Income divided by the sales price equals the capitalization rate.
Thus,

NOI / SP = Cap Rate

NOI	/ (Divided)	Sales Price	Equals	Cap Rate
$100,000	/	$850,000	=	11.7%
$95,000	/	$800,000	=	11.8%
$90,000	/	$750,000	=	12%
$85,000	/	$700,000	=	12.1%
			Indicated Cap Rate	11.7% - 12.1%

Therefore a NOI of $100,000 and a capitalization rate of 12% is indicated. Thus, $100,000 / .12 = $833,333. Now for the residential income approach method, let's look at how you do this approach.

Formula for the Income Capitalization Approach

Commercial			
Income Capitalization Approach	NOI Net Operating Income This is income after operating expenses have been paid.	/ Cap Rate This is the return on and of the investment.	= Income Capitalization Approach to Value.
Example	$100,000	/ 8	= $1,250,000
	$100,000	/ 10	= $1,000,000

Residential Income Approach

Gross Rent Multiplier

GRM = Gross Monthly Multiplier. This was previously labeled gross monthly rent multiplier.

The first step is to acquire comparable sales that were rented at the time of sale. The formula is sales price divided by the gross monthly rent. Thus, sales price / gross rent = GRM.

Thus, $200,000 (sales price / $2,000 (monthly rent) = 100 GRM. This also indicates how many months it will take the investor to receive her money back on a gross basis.

Now that you understand the GRM method, let's review the GIM method as illustrated on the following chart. This also indicates how many years it will take the investor to receive her money back on a gross basis.

Gross Income Multiplier

The GIM (Gross Income Multiplier) method works very much like the GRM; however, the GIM is based on annual income. Thus, $3,000,000 (sales price) / $285,000 (gross annual income) = 10.53.

Life estates: A life estate is a freehold estate that will lasts as long as a specified person lives.

Undivided interest in commonly held property: This type of ownership is shared by multiply owners.

Easements: An easement is the right to use another property for a period of time. They can be permanent or temporary. Also, easements can be attached to a person or the land itself.

Timeshares: A timeshare is a right to use a property for a specific period of time. They can be for 1 week or more.

Cooperatives: When you purchase shares of stock in a corporation and that corporation owns a building and you receive a priority lease for a particular unit, you have purchased part of a cooperative.

Leased fee estate: A leased fee estate is owned by an owner. The purchaser receives a fee simple estate when the close. Then they sign a lease that creates a leased fee estate. They have in effect leased their fee.

Leasehold estate: A leasehold estate is the estate enjoyed by the tenant. After signing a lease with the landlord, the tenant receives a leasehold estate.

Partial Interest: A partial interest is something less than 100 percent interest. For example, when doing an appraisal, the appraiser starts with the whole bundle of rights that include the right to sell, right to lease, right to improve, right to do nothing.

Preamble: The purpose of the *Uniform Standards of Professional Appraisal Practice* (USPAP) is to promote and maintain a high level of public trust in appraisal practice by establishing requirements for appraisers. It is essential that appraisers develop and communicate their analyses, opinions, and conclusions to intended users of their services in a manner that is meaningful and not misleading. Source: Appraisal Foundation, USPAP.

Standards and Standards Rules:

SR-1	Real Property Appraisal: Development
SR-2	Real Property Appraisal: Reporting
SR-3	Appraisal Review: Development and Reporting
SR-4	Real Property Appraisal Consulting: Development
SR-5	Real Property Appraisal Consulting: Reporting
SR-6	Mass Appraisal: Development and Reporting

Statement on Standards: These are statements that are part of USPAP and have the full weight of a standards Rule. Their purpose is to clarify, interpret, explain or elaborate on USPAP.

Advisory Opinions: These opinions are guidance from the ASB (Appraisal Standards Board) that do not change USPAP, nor are they actually part of the standards. They are simply a way of receiving advice from the ASB on the standards.

Extraordinary Assumption: This is an unknown issue in regard to the appraisal. Let's pretend you are appraising a property that has a few cracks in the sheetrock as well as the brick and mortar. You can note the items and make an extraordinary assumption that the improvements are performing the function for which they were intended. Another example of using an extraordinary assumption is when you do not receive a copy of the sales contract. You could use an extraordinary assumption that the sales price and terms are correct based on the information that you received.

Hypothetical Condition: If you are appraising an office building that has not been started. You could appraise the building based on the hypothetical condition that it is complete. So, when using a hypothetical condition, you are assuming that a fact that is untrue to be true.

Ethics Rule: There are four sections of the ethics rule. These include conduct, management, confidentiality and record keeping.

Conduct: An appraiser must not behave in criminal conduct. An appraiser must perform assignments impartially, objectively and independently.

Management: The payment of undisclosed fees is unethical. An appraiser cannot base an appraisal on a predetermined result. Appraisers should not advertise in a misleading manner.

Confidentiality: If your client advises you to keep the fact that he is purchasing a property confidential, then you must keep it confidential. If you appraise a house located at 510 Elm Street for Wells Fargo and next week Wachovia contacts you regarding the same property and borrower. You indicate that you just appraised the property for another lender and same borrower. You have just violated the confidentiality section of USPAP. You could appraise the property without violating USPAP, but you will need to set up a new file with current information from the lender. In other words, you need a new appraisal request and contract to perform the appraisal assignment.

Record Keeping: This is one of the most confused sections of USPAP, (Based on my experience). You must keep a copy of the appraisal and work file for a minimum of five years or two years after the final disposition of a court case. The copy can be saved via paper or electronic.

Appraiser

An appraiser according to USPAP/2010-2011 states "one who is expected to perform valuation services competently and in a manner that is independent, impartial and objective." Source: USPAP, Appraisal Foundation.

Sources Cited

Www.appraisalinstitute.org

The FHA and VA Appraiser: Thriving and Surviving, 2007, Timothy Detty, Hondros Learning, Watersville, OH.

www.craigjulian.com

Dictionary of Real Estate Appraisal 4th Edition, July, 2002, Appraisal Institute, Chicago, IL.

www.fha.gov

www.hud.gov

http://www.inspectapedia.com

Uniform Standards of Professional Appraisal Practice, (USPAP), 2008-2009, Appraisal Foundation, Washington, DC, www.Appraisalfoundation.org

Answers to the challenges

Chapter Two

Quiz Challenge

1. Do I reject a house if it is not hooked up to public utilities and they are available? **No, you report what is available and the underwriter will make the decision to hook up or not.**

2. HUD/FHA expects me to deduct all seller concessions when they are paid by the seller: – T or **F**. HUD/FHA expects the appraiser to only deduct for sales concessions when they affect the sale of the comparable.

3. HUD expects you to be conservative when completing appraisal assignments – T or **F**.

4. HUD/FHA expects you to error on the side of caution in regard to repairs

   T or **F**.

Chapter Three

Case Study Challenge

Case Study 1

Based on the following photo, would this road pass the test? No. The road consists of dirt and is not an all weather road. The FHA requirement is an all weather road in all four seasons. Thus, the report would be subject to an all weather road be completed.

Case Study 2

Based on the following photo, would you make a note or complete the report subject to? I would complete the report "as is". This brick is performing for which it was intended; however, it does have some flaws.

Case Study 3

Based on the following photo, would you make it to subject to or just note the item in the report? This is a photo of rotted wood. If the rooted wood is not repaired, further damage will happen over time. Therefore, I would make the report subject to repair of the rotted wood.

Chapter Five

Challenge/Quiz

1. What are the three S's again? Safety, Security and Soundness.

2. What about well and septic again? In other words, what should I observe in regard to a water well and septic tank? You will check for corrosion and distances from the septic field to the water well.

Chapter Six

Challenge/Quiz

1. Subject to repair as it has rotted wood.

2. Subject to hand rails being installed as this is a safety concern.

3. You need the following items: Gather information from the HUD Data plate: 1. Name and address of the plant; 2. Serial number, model designation, and date built. (If the data plate is missing, you can make the appraisal subject to providing the information to the underwriter. This information can be obtained from www.ibts.org/label 3. Permanent Foundation (Need engineer's certification). The engineers certification should be in the appraisal report. A plastic skirt is allowed to be around the foundation; however, the actual foundation must be concrete, treated wood, etc. 4. Towing and hitches must be removed. 5. Must have utility connection. 6. GLA must be at least 400 square feet. 7. If any additions have been made, then another structural report will be required for safety compliance.

4. Subject to repair as it looks yucky.

5. Subject to as this is a soundness issue. It looks like it would not last very long.

6. This is a busy road and therefore a security issue. This property would not be marketable if HUD/FHA has to take it back.

7. Subject to a new roof.

8. This property has excess land. Be careful when valuing the lot for the subject.

9. This house most likely has functional obsolescence as it lacks functional utility. Of course the test will be the market.

10. You will need plans and specifications to complete this appraisal.

11. This house has too many angles and you should avoid such problems. I am just kidding, but be careful when measuring.

www.ingramcontent.com/pod-product-compliance
Lightning Source LLC
Chambersburg PA
CBHW080426270326
41929CB00018B/3177